NEWSPAPER DAYS

Maryland Paperback Bookshelf

Publisher's Note

Works published as part of the Maryland Paperback Bookshelf are, we like to think, books that are classics of a kind. While some social attitudes have changed and knowledge of our surroundings has increased, we believe that the value of these books as literature, as history, and as timeless perspectives on our region remains undiminished.

NEWSPAPER

DAYS

1899-1906

H. L. MENCKEN

The Johns Hopkins University Press

Baltimore and London

Some of these chapters have appeared, either wholly or in part, in the *New Yorker*. The author offers his thanks to the editors of that magazine for permission to reprint them.

Originally published in a hardcover edition by Alfred A. Knopf, New York
Published by arrangement with Alfred A. Knopf, Inc.
Maryland Paperback Bookshelf edition, 1996
05 04 03 02 01 00 99 98 97 96   5 4 3 2 1

The Johns Hopkins University Press
2715 North Charles Street
Baltimore, Maryland 21218-4319
The Johns Hopkins Press Ltd., London

Library of Congress Cataloging-in-Publication Data will be found at the end of this book.

A catalog record for this book is available from the British Library.

ISBN 0-8018-5340-0 (pbk.)

Frontispiece: H. L. Mencken in the back yard at 1524 Hollins Street, 1902. Photograph courtesy of the Enoch Pratt Free Library.

TABLE OF

CONTENTS

PREFACE

THE RECOLLECTIONS here embalmed, I should say at once, have nothing in common with the high, astounding tales of journalistic derring-do that had a considerable run several years ago, after the devourers of best-sellers had begun to tire of medical memoirs. In the second half of the period here covered I became a city editor, which is to say, a fellow of high mightiness in a newspaper office, and at the very end I was lifted by one of fate's ironies into even higher dignities, but the narrative has principally to do with my days as a reporter, when I was young, goatish and full of an innocent delight in the world. My adventures in that character, save maybe in one or two details, were hardly extraordinary; on the contrary they seem to me now, looking back upon them nostalgically, to have been marked by an excess of normalcy. Nevertheless, they had their moments — in fact, they were

made up, subjectively, of one continuous, unrelent-
ing, almost delirious moment — and when I re-
vive them now it is mainly to remind myself and
inform historians that a newspaper reporter, in
those remote days, had a grand and gaudy time of
it, and no call to envy any man.

In the long, busy years following I had experiences of a more profound and even alarming nature, and if the mood were on me I could fill a book
with inside stuff almost fit to match the high,
astounding tales aforesaid. I roamed, in the practise of my trade, from the river Jordan in the East
to Hollywood in the West, and from the Orkney
Islands in the North to Morocco and the Spanish
Main in the South, and, like every other journalist,
I met, listened to and smelled all sorts of magnifi-
coes, including Presidents and Vice-Presidents,
generals and admirals, bishops and archbishops,
murderers and murderesses, geniuses both scientific
and literary, movie and stage stars, heavyweight
champions of the world, Class A and Class B royal-
ties, judges and hangmen, millionaires and labor
goons, and vast hordes of other notables, including
most of the recognized Cæsars and Shakespeares of
journalism. I edited both newspapers and magazines, some of them successes and some of them not,
and got a close, confidential view of the manner in
which opinion is formulated and merchanted on
this earth. My own contributions to the mess ran
to millions of words, and I came to know intimately

many of its most revered confectioners. More than
once I have staggered out of editorial conferences
dripping cold sweat, and wondering dizzily how
God got along for so many years without the *New
Republic* and the Manchester *Guardian*. And at
other times I have marvelled that the human race
did not revolt against the imposture, dig up the
carcass of Johann Gutenberg, and heave it to the
buzzards and hyenas in some convenient zoo.

A newspaper man in active practise finds it hard
to remain a mere newspaper man: he is constantly
beset by temptations to try other activities, and if
he manages to resist them it takes a kind of forti-
tude that less protean men, badgered only by their
hormones and their creditors, never have need of.
I was born, happily, with no more public spirit
than a cat, and have thus found it relatively easy
to throw off all the commoner lures, but there have
been times when the sirens fetched me clearly below
the belt, and I did some wobbling. In 1912, though
no one will ever believe it, I was groomed surrep-
titiously as a dark horse for the Democratic Vice-
Presidential nomination, and if one eminent American statesman, X, had not got tight at the last
minute, and another, Y, kept unaccountably sober,
I might have become immortal. Two years later I
was offered $30,000 cash, deposited in bank to my
order, to write anti-Prohibition speeches for the
illiterates in the two Houses of Congress. A little
further on an Episcopal bishop asked me to tackle

and try to throw a nascent convert, female and rich, who had thrice slipped out of his hands at the very brink of the font. Another time the prophet of a new religion, then very prosperous in the Middle West, offered to consecrate me as a bishop myself, with power to bind and loose; and almost simultaneously I was arrested on Boston Common on a charge of vending obscene literature to the young gentlemen of Harvard. I have seen something of the horrors of war, and much too much of the worse horrors of peace. On five several occasions I have been offered the learned degree of *legum doctor*, though few men are less learned in the law than I am, or have less respect for it; and at other times I have been invited to come in and be lynched by the citizens of three of the great Christian states of the Union.

Such prodigies and monstrosities I could pile up for hours, along with a lot of instructive blabbing about what this or that immortal once told me off the record, for I have had the honor of encountering three Presidents of the United States in their cups, not to mention sitting Governors of all the states save six. But I bear in mind Sir Thomas Overbury's sneer at the fellow who " chooseth rather to be counted a spy than not a politician, and maintains his reputation by naming great men familiarly," and so hold my peace: let some larval Ph.D. dig the dirt out of my papers marked " Strictly Private: Destroy Unread " after I shove off for bliss eternal. In the present book my only purpose is to try to recreate for myself, and for any one who may care to follow me, the gaudy life that young newspaper reporters led in the major American cities at the turn of the century. I believed then, and still believe today, that it was the maddest, gladdest, damndest existence ever enjoyed by mortal youth. At a time when the respectable bourgeois youngsters of my generation were college freshmen, oppressed by simian sophomores and affronted with balderdash daily and hourly by chalky pedagogues, I was at large in a wicked seaport of half a million people, with a front seat at every public show, as free of the night as of the day, and getting earfuls and eyefuls of instruction in a hundred giddy arcana, none of them taught in schools. On my twenty-first birthday, by all orthodox cultural standards, I probably reached my all-time low, for the heavy reading of my teens had been abandoned in favor of life itself, and I did not return seriously to the lamp until a time near the end of this record. But it would be an exaggeration to say that I was ignorant, for if I neglected the humanities I was meanwhile laying in all the worldly wisdom of a police lieutenant, a bartender, a shyster lawyer, or a midwife. And it would certainly be idiotic to say that I was not happy. The illusion that swathes and bedizens journalism, bringing in its endless squads of recruits, was still full upon me, and I had yet to taste the sharp teeth of responsibility. Life was arduous, but it was gay and carefree. The days chased one another like kittens chasing their tails.

Whether or not the young journalists of today live so spaciously is a question that I am not competent to answer, for my contacts with them, of late years, have been rather scanty. They undoubtedly get a great deal more money than we did in 1900, but their freedom is much less than ours was, and they somehow give me the impression, seen at a distance, of complacency rather than intrepidity. In my day a reporter who took an assignment was wholly on his own until he got back to the office, and even then he was little molested until his copy was turned in at the desk; today he tends to become only a homunculus at the end of a telephone wire, and the reduction of his observations to prose is commonly farmed out to literary castrati who never leave the office, and hence never feel the wind of the world in their faces or see anything with their own eyes. I well recall my horror when I heard, for the first time, of a journalist who had laid in a pair of what were then called bicycle pants and taken to golf: it was as if I had encountered a studhorse with his hair done up in frizzes, and pink bowknots peeking out of them. It seemed, in some vague way, ignominious, and even a bit indelicate. I was shocked almost as much when I first heard of reporters joining labor unions, and describing themselves as wage slaves. The underlying ideology here, of course, was anything but new, for I doubt that there has ever been a competent reporter in history who did not regard the proprietors of his paper as sordid rascals, all dollars and no sense. But it is one thing (*a*) to curl the lip over such wretches, and quite another thing (*b*) to bellow and beat the breast under their atrocities, just as it is one thing (a^2) to sass a cruel city editor with, so to speak, the naked hands, and another thing (b^2) to confront him from behind a phalanx of government agents and labor bravoes. The *a* operations are easy to reconcile with the old-time journalist's concept of himself as a free spirit and darling of the gods, licensed by his high merits to ride and deride the visible universe; the *b*'s must suggest inevitably a certain unhappy self-distrust, perhaps not without ground.

Like its companion volume, " Happy Days " (1940) this book is mainly true, but with occasional stretchers. I have checked my recollections whenever possible, and found them reasonably accurate. For the rest, I must throw myself upon the bosom of that " friendly and judicious reader " to whom Charles Lamb dedicated the Essays of Elia — that understanding fellow, male or female, who refuses to take " everything perversely in the absolute and literal sense," but gives it " a fair construction, as to an after-dinner conversation."

BALTIMORE, 1941.   H. L. M.

NEWSPAPER DAYS

I

ALLEGRO

CON BRIO

My father died on Friday, January 13, 1899, and was buried on the ensuing Sunday. On the Monday evening immediately following, having shaved with care and put on my best suit of clothes, I presented myself in the city-room of the old Baltimore *Morning Herald*, and applied to Max Ways, the city editor, for a job on his staff. I was eighteen years, four months and four days old, wore my hair longish and parted in the middle, had on a high stiff collar and an Ascot cravat, and weighed something on the minus side of 120 pounds. I was thus hardly a spectacle to exhilarate a city editor, but Max was an amiable fellow and that night he was in an extra-amiable mood, for (as he told me afterward) there was a good dinner under his belt, with a couple of globes of malt to wash it down, and all of his reporters, so far as he was aware, were transiently sober. So he received me very politely, and even cordially. Had I any newspaper experience? The reply, alas, had to be no. What was my education? I was a graduate of the Baltimore Polytechnic. What considerations had turned my fancy toward the newspaper business? All that I could say was that it seemed to be a sort of celestial call: I was busting with literary ardors and had been writing furiously for what, at eighteen, was almost an age — maybe four, or even five years. Writing what — prose or verse? Both. Anything published? I had to play dead here, for my bibliography, to date, was confined to a couple of anonymous poems in the Baltimore *American* — a rival paper, and hence probably not admired.

Max looked me over ruminatively — I had been standing all the while — and made the reply that city editors had been making to young aspirants since the days of the first Washington hand-press. There was, unhappily, no vacancy on the staff. He would take my name, and send for me in case some catastrophe unforeseen — and, as I gathered, almost unimaginable — made one. I must have drooped visibly, for the kindly Max at once thought of something better. Did I have a job? Yes, I was working for my Uncle Henry, now the sole heir and assign of my father's old tobacco firm of Aug. Mencken & Bro. Well, I had better keep that job, but maybe it might be an idea for me to drop in now and then of an evening, say between seven thirty and seven forty-five. Nothing, of course, could be promised ; in fact, the odds against anything turning up were appalling. But if I would present myself at appropriate intervals there might be a chance, if it were God's will, to try me out, soon or late, on something commensurate with my undemonstrated talents. Such trial flights, it was unnecessary to mention, carried no emolument. They added a lot to a city editor's already heavy cargo of cares and anxieties, and out of the many that were called only a few were ever chosen.

I retired nursing a mixture of disappointment and elation, but with the elation quickly besting the disappointment — and the next night, precisely at seven thirty-one, I was back. Max waved me away without parley : he was busy jawing an office-boy. The third night he simply shook his head, and so on the fourth, fifth, sixth and seventh. On the eighth — or maybe it was the ninth or tenth — he motioned me to wait while he finished thumbing through a pile of copy, and then asked suddenly : " Do you ever read the *Herald* ? " When I answered yes, he followed with " What do you think of it ? " This one had all the appearance of a trap, and my heart missed a couple of beats, but the holy saints were with me. " I think," I said, " that it is much better written than the *Sunpaper*." I was to learn later that Max smelled something artful here, but, as always, he held himself well, and all I could observe was the faint flutter of a smile across his face. At length he spoke. " Come back," he said, " tomorrow night."

I came back, you may be sure — and found him missing, for he had forgotten that it was his night off. The next night I was there again — and found him too busy to notice me. And so the night following, and the next, and the next. To make an end, this went on for four weeks, night in and night out, Mondays, Tuesdays, Wednesdays, Thursdays, Fridays, Saturdays and Sundays. A tremendous blizzard came down upon Baltimore, and for a couple of days the trolley-cars were stalled, but I hoofed it ever hopefully to the *Herald* office, and then hoofed it sadly home. There arrived eventually, after what seemed a geological epoch by my calendar, the evening of Thursday, February 23, 1899. I found Max reading copy, and for a few minutes he did not see me. Then his eyes lifted, and he said casually : " Go out to Govanstown, and see if anything is happening there. We are supposed to have a Govanstown correspondent, but he hasn't been heard from for six days."

The percussion must have been tremendous, for I remember nothing about getting to Govanstown. It is now a part of Baltimore, but in 1899 it was only a country village, with its own life and tribulations. No cop was in sight when I arrived, but I found the volunteer firemen playing pinochle in their engine-house. The blizzard had blockaded their front door with a drift fifteen feet high, but they had dug themselves out, and were now lathering for a fire, though all the water-plugs in the place were still frozen. They had no news save their hopes. Across the glacier of a street I saw two lights — a bright one in a drugstore and a dim one in a funeral parlor. The undertaker, like nearly all the rest of Govanstown, was preparing to go to bed, and when I routed him out and he came downstairs in his pants and undershirt it was only to say that he had no professional business in hand. The druggist, hugging a red-hot egg-stove behind his colored bottles, was more productive. The town cop, he said, had just left in a two-horse buggy to assist in a horse-stealing case at Kingsville, a long drive out the Belair pike, and the Improved Order of Red Men had postponed their oyster-supper until March 6. When I got back to the *Herald* office, along toward eleven o'clock, Max instructed me to forget the Red Men and write the horse-stealing. There was a vacant desk in a far corner, and at it, for ten minutes, I wrote and tore up, wrote and tore up. Finally there emerged the following:

A horse, a buggy and several sets of harness, valued in all at about $250, were stolen last night from the stable of Howard Quinlan, near Kingsville. The county police are at work on the case, but so far no trace of either thieves or booty has been found.

Max gave only a grunt to my copy, but as I was leaving the office, exhausted but exultant, he called me back, and handed me a letter to the editor demanding full and friendly publicity, on penalty of a boycott, for an exhibition of what was then called a kinetoscope or cineograph. " A couple of lines," he said, " will be enough. Nearly everybody has seen a cineograph by now." I wrote:

At Otterbein Memorial U.B. Church, Roland and Fifth avenues, Hampden, Charles H. Stanley and J. Albert Loose entertained a large audience last night with an exhibition of war scenes by the cineograph.

I was up with the milkman the next morning to search the paper, and when I found both of my pieces, exactly as written, there ran such thrills through my system as a barrel of brandy and 100,-000 volts of electricity could not have matched. Somehow or other I must have done my duty by Aug. Mencken & Bro., for my uncle apparently noticed nothing, but certainly my higher cerebral centers were not focussed on them. That night I got to the *Herald* office so early that Max had not come back from dinner. When he appeared he looked me over thoughtfully, and suggested that it might be a good plan to try my talents on a village adjacent to Govanstown, Waverly by name. It was, he observed, a poor place, full of Methodists and Baptists who seldom cut up, but now and then a horse ran away or a pastor got fired. Reaching it after a long search in the snow, and raking it

from end to end, I turned up two items — one an
Epworth League entertainment, and the other a
lecture for nearby farmers, by title (I have the
clipping before me), " Considering the Present
Low Price of Hay, Would It Not Be Advisable to
Lessen the Acreage of Hay for Market? " Max
showed no enthusiasm for either, but after I had
finished writing them he handed me an amateur
press-agent's handout about a new Quaker school
and directed me to rewrite it. It made twenty-
eight lines in the paper next morning, and lifted me
beyond the moon to Orion. On the night following
Max introduced me to two or three reporters, and
told them that I was a youngster trying for a job.
My name, he said, was Macon. They greeted me
with considerable reserve.

Of the weeks following I recall definitely but
one thing — that I never seemed to get enough
sleep. I was expected to report at the cigar factory of Aug. Mencken & Bro. at eight o'clock every
morning, which meant that I had to turn out at
seven. My day there ran officially to five thirty,
but not infrequently my uncle detained me to talk
about family affairs, for my father had died intes-
tate and his estate was in process of administration, with two sets of lawyers discovering mare's
nests from time to time. Thus it was often six
o'clock before I escaped, and in the course of the
next hour or so I had to get home, change my
clothes, bolt my dinner, and return downtown to

the *Herald* office. For a couple of weeks Max kept me at my harrying of the remoter suburbs — a job, as I afterward learned, as distasteful to ripe reporters as covering a fashionable church-wedding or a convention of the W.C.T.U. I ranged from Catonsville in the far west to Back River in the east, and from Tuxedo Park in the north to Mt. Winans in the south. Hour after hour I rode the suburban trolleys, and one night, as I recall uncomfortably over all these years, my fares at a nickel a throw came to sixty cents, which was more than half my day's pay from Aug. Mencken & Bro. Max had said nothing about an expense account, and I was afraid to ask. Once, returning from a dismal village called Gardenville, a mile or two northeast of the last electric light, I ventured to ask him how far my diocese ran in that direction. "You are supposed to keep on out the road," he said, "until you meet the Philadelphia reporters coming in." This was an ancient Baltimore newspaper wheeze, but it was new to me, and I was to enjoy it a great deal better when I heard it worked off on my successors.

But my exploration of the fringes of Baltimore, though it came near being exhaustive, was really not long drawn out, for in a little while Max began to hand me city assignments of the kind that no one else wanted — installations of new evangelical pastors, meetings of wheelmen, interviews with bores just back from Europe, the Klondike or

Oklahoma, orgies of one sort or another at the Y.M.C.A., minor political rallies, concerts, funerals, and so on. Most of my early clippings perished in the great Baltimore fire of 1904, but a few survived, and I find from them that I covered a number of stories that would seem as antediluvian today as a fight between two brontosauri — for example, the showing of a picture-play by Alexander Black (a series of lantern-slides with a thin thread of banal recitative), and a chalk-talk by Frank Beard. When it appeared that I knew something of music, I was assigned to a long series of organ recitals in obscure churches, vocal and instrumental recitals in even more obscure halls, and miscellaneous disturbances of the peace in lodge-rooms and among the German singing societies. Within the space of two weeks I heard one violinist, then very popular in Baltimore, play Raff's Cavatina no less than eight times. The *Herald's* music critic in those days, an Englishman named W. G. Owst, was a very indolent fellow, and when he discovered that I could cover such uproars without making any noticeable bulls, he saw to it that I got more and more of them. Finally, I was entrusted with an assault upon Mendelssohn's " Elijah " by the Baltimore Oratorio Society — and suffered a spasm of stage fright that was cured by dropping into the Pratt Library before the performance, and doing a little precautionary reading.

Thus the Winter ran into Spring, and I began

to think of myself as almost a journalist. So far, to be sure, I had been entrusted with no spot news, and Max had never sent me out to help a regular member of the staff, but he was generous with his own advice, and I quickly picked up the jargon and ways of thought of the city-room. In this acclimatization I was aided by the device that had helped me to fathom Mendelssohn's " Elijah " and has always been my recourse in time of difficulty: what I couldn't learn otherwise I tried to learn by reading. Unhappily, the almost innumerable texts on journalism that now serve aspirants were then still unwritten, and I could find, in fact, only one formal treatise on the subject at the Pratt Library. It was " Steps Into Journalism," by E. L. Shuman of the Chicago *Tribune*, and though it was a primitive in its class it was very clearly and sensibly written, and I got a great deal of useful information out of it. Also, I read all of the newspaper fiction then on paper — for example, Richard Harding Davis's " Gallegher and Other Stories," Jesse Lynch Williams's " The Stolen Story and Other Stories," and Elizabeth G. Jordan's " Tales of the City-Room," the last two of which had but lately come out.[1]

How I found time for this reading I can't tell

[1] It must have been a little later that I read " With Kitchener to Khartoum," " From Capetown to Ladysmith " and the other books of George W. Steevens, of the London *Mail*. They made a powerful impression on me, and I still believe that Steevens was the greatest newspaper reporter who ever lived.

you, for I was kept jumping by my two jobs, but find it I did. One night, sitting in the city-room waiting for an assignment, I fell asleep, and the thoughtful Max suggested that I take one night off a week, and mentioned Sunday. The next Sunday I stayed in bed until noon, and returned to it at 8 p.m., and thereafter I was ready for anything. As the Spring drifted on my assignments grew better and better, and when the time came for high-school commencements I covered all of them. There were five in those days, beginning with that of the City College and ending with that of the Colored High-school, and I heard the Mayor of Baltimore unload precisely the same speech at each. Max, who knew the man, complimented me on making his observations sound different every time, and even more or less intelligent, and I gathered the happy impression that my days as an unpaid volunteer were nearing their end. But a city editor of that costive era, at least in Baltimore, could take on a new man only by getting rid of an old one, and for a month or so longer I had to wait. Finally, some old-timer or other dropped out, and my time had come. Max made a little ceremony of my annunciation, though no one else was present. My salary, he said, would be $7 a week, with the hope of an early lift to $8 if I made good. I would have the use of a book of passes on the trolley-cars, and might turn in expense-accounts to cover any actual outlays. There was, at the moment, no typewriter available for me, but he had hopes of extracting one from Nachman, the business manager, in the near future. This was followed by some good advice. *Imprimis*, never trust a cop: whenever possible, verify his report. *Item*, always try to get in early copy: the first story to reach the city-desk has a much better chance of being printed in full than the last. *Item*, be careful about dates, names, ages, addresses, figures of every sort. *Item*, keep in mind at all times the dangers of libel. Finally, don't be surprised if you go to a house for information, and are invited to lift it from the *Sun* of the next morning. " The *Sun* is the Bible of Baltimore, and has almost a monopoly on many kinds of news. But don't let that fact discourage you. You can get it too if you dig hard enough, and always remember this: any *Herald* reporter who is worth a damn can write rings around a *Sun* reporter."

This last was very far from literally true, as I was to discover when I came to cover stories in competition with such *Sun* reporters as Dorsey Guy and Harry West, but there was nevertheless a certain plausibility in it, for the *Sun* laid immense stress upon accuracy, and thus fostered a sober, matter-of-fact style in its men. The best of them burst through those trammels, but the rank and file tended to write like bookkeepers. As for Max, he greatly favored a more imaginative and colorful manner. He had been a very good reporter himself, with not only a hand for humor but also a

14

trick of pathos, and he tried to inspire his slaves to the same. Not many of them were equal to the business, but all of them save a few poor old automata tried, and as a result the *Herald* was rather briskly written, and its general direction was toward the New York *Sun*, then still scintillating under the impulse of Charles A. Dana, rather than toward the Baltimore *Sun* and the *Congressional Record*. It was my good fortune, during my first week on the staff, to turn up the sort of story that Max liked especially — the sudden death of a colored street preacher on the street, in the midst of a hymn. I was not present at the ringside, and had to rely on the cops for the facts, but I must have got a touch of drama into my report, for Max was much pleased, and gave me, as a reward, a pass to a performance of Rose Sydell's London Blondes.

I had gathered from the newspaper fiction mentioned a few pages back that the typical American city editor was a sort of cross between an ice-wagon driver and a fire-alarm, " full of strange oaths " and imprecations, and given to firing whole files of men at the drop of a hat. But if that monster actually existed in the Republic, it was surely not in the Baltimore *Herald* office. Max, of course, was decently equipped for his art and mystery: he could swear loudly enough on occasion and had a pretty hand for shattering invective, but most of the time, even when he was sorely tried, he kept to good humor and was polite to one and all. Whenever I made a mess of a story, which was certainly often enough, he summoned me to his desk and pointed out my blunders. When I came in with a difficult story, confused and puzzled, he gave me quick and clear directions, and they always straightened me out. Observing his operations with the sharp eyes of youth, I began to understand the curious equipment required of a city editor. He had to be an incredible amalgam of army officer and literary critic, diplomat and jail warden, psychologist and fortune-teller. If he could not see around corners and through four or five feet of brick he was virtually blind, and if he could not hear overtones audible normally only to dogs and children he was almost deaf. His knowledge of his town, as he gathered experience, combined that of a police captain, an all-night hackman, and a priest in a rowdy parish. He was supposed to know the truth about everyone and everything, even though he seldom printed it, and one of his most useful knowledges — in fact, he used it every day — was his knowledge of the most probable whereabouts of every person affected with a public interest, day or night.

Max had these skills, and many more. How he would have made out on the larger papers of a later period, with their incessant editions, I do not attempt to guess, but in his time and place he was a very competent man, and had the respect as well as the affection of his staff. In person he was of middle height, with light hair that was beginning to fall out, and an equator that had already begun to bulge. What remained of his hair he wore longish, in what was then called the football style. He affected rolling collars, and sometimes wore a Windsor tie. His colored shirts, in the manner of the day, were ironed to shine like glass, and his clothes were of somewhat advanced cut. We younger reporters modelled ourselves upon him in dress as in mien. The legends that played about him were mainly not of a professional nature, but romantic. He was a bachelor, and was supposed to be living in sin with a beautiful creature who occasionally took a drop too much, and exposed him to the embarrassment of her caterwauling. Whether or not that creature had any actual existence I can't tell you: all I can say is that I never saw her, and that the only time I ever visited Max in his quarters (he was laid up with pink-eye) I found him living *a cappella* upstairs of a French restaurant, and waited on by the proprietor's well-seasoned and far from aphrodisiac wife.[2]

It was a pleasant office that I found myself en-

[2] When he quit the *Herald* Max went into politics, and lived to be one of the Democratic bosses of Baltimore. But the first time he ran for elective office he was beaten, mainly, so it was reported, because many voters assumed from his name that he was a Jew, and others suspected that he might even be a Chinaman. He was actually of Scotch-Irish, Welsh, English and Pennsylvania German stock. He later married the charming secretary of the Governor of Maryland, and became the father of a son and a daughter who followed him into the newspaper business. He died in 1923.

tering. Many of the reporters, to be sure, were rummy old-timers who were of small ability and no diligence, but they were all at least amiable fellows, and working beside them were some youngsters of superior quality. The *Herald* Building was new, and its fifth-floor city-room was one of the most comfortable and convenient that I have ever seen, even to this day. But in many respects it would seem primitive now: it had, for example, but two telephones — one belonging to each of the two companies that then fought for subscribers in Baltimore. Both were Paleozoic instruments attached to the wall, and no one ever used them if it could be avoided. There was no telephone on the city editor's desk until my own time in that office, beginning in 1903. The office library, save for a dog's-eared encyclopedia with several volumes missing, was made up wholly of government reports, and the only man who ever used it was an old fellow who had the job of compiling cattle and provision prices. He finished work every day at about 5 p.m. and spent an hour reading in the encyclopedia. There was no index of the paper, and no office morgue. The city editor kept a clipping file of his own, and when it failed him he had to depend upon the shaky memories of the older reporters.

The city staff, save for such early birds as the court reporter, came to work at half an hour after noon, and every man was responsible for his baili-wick until 11 at night. The city editor himself began work an hour earlier and worked an hour or so later. There were no bulldogs or other early editions. The first mail edition did not close until after midnight. In consequence, there was no hurry about getting stories on paper, except very late ones. Rewrite men were unheard of. Every reporter, no matter how remote the scene of his story, came back to the office and wrote it himself. If he lagged, his copy was taken from him page by page, and he was urged on by the grunting and growling of the city editor, who was his own chief copy-reader, and usually wrote the head on the leading local story of the night. A great deal of copy was still written by hand, for there were not enough typewriters in the office to go round, and every time Nachman, the business manager, was asked to buy another he went on like a man stabbed with poniards. But every reporter had a desk, and every desk was equipped with a spittoon. This was a great convenience to me, for I had acquired the sinful habit of tobacco-chewing in my father's cigar factory, and am, in fact, still more or less in its loathsome toils.

The office was kept pretty clean by Bill Christian, a barber who had got the job of building superintendent because Colonel Cunningham, the managing editor, liked his tonsorial touch. Bill was allergic to work himself, but he rode herd diligently on his staff of colored scavengers, and the whole editorial floor was strangely spick and span for that time. Even the colonel's own den was excavated at least twice a month, and its accumulation of discarded newspapers hauled out. Bill failed, however, to make any progress against the army of giant cockroaches that had moved in when the building was opened, three or four years before. On dull nights the copy-readers would detail office-boys to corral half a dozen of these monsters, and then race them across the city-room floor, guiding them with walking-sticks. The sport required some skill, for if a jockey pressed his nag too hard he was apt to knock off its hind legs.

II

DRILL FOR A

ROOKIE

MY first regular assignment as a reporter was
South Baltimore, or, to speak technically, the
Southern police district. It was, as I shall remark
again in Chapter XVIII, a big territory, and there
was always something doing in it, but though my
memories of it are copious and melodramatic, I
must have spent only a few weeks in it, for by the
end of the Spring, as I find by a promenade
through the *Herald's* files, I was covering Afra-
merican razor-parties in the Northwestern, which
was almost as black as Mississippi, and making occasional dips into the Western, which embraced
the largest and busiest of Baltimore's five Tender-
loins.

In those days a reporter who had durable legs

and was reasonably sober tended to see a varied service, for it was not unusual for one of his elders to succumb to the jug and do a vanishing act. More than once during my first weeks, after turning in my own budget of assaults, fires, drownings and other such events from the Southern, I was sent out at eleven o'clock at night to find a lost colleague of the Eastern or Northeastern, and pump his news out of him, if he had any. It was by the same route, in July, that I found myself promoted to the Central, which was the premier Baltimore district, journalistically speaking, for it included the busiest of the police courts, a downtown hospital, police headquarters, the city jail, and the morgue. The regular man there had turned up at the office one noon so far gone in rum that Max relieved him of duty, and I was gazetted to his place as a means of shaming him, for I was still the youngest reporter in the office. When he continued in his cups the day following I was retained as his *locum tenens,* and when he went on to a third day he was reduced to the Northern police district, the Siberia of Baltimore, and I found myself his heir.

This man, though we eventually became good friends, resented his demotion so bitterly that for weeks he refused to speak to me, but I was too busy in my new bailiwick to pay any attention to him. Its police court was the liveliest in town, and had the smartest and most colorful magistrate, Gene Grannan by name. He was always willing to help the press by developing the dramatic content of the cases before him, and during my first week he thus watered and manured for me a couple of stories that delighted Max, and boosted my own stock. Such stories were almost a *Herald* monopoly, for *Sun* reporters were hobbled by their paper's craze for mathematical accuracy, and most *American* reporters were too stupid to recognize good stuff when they saw it. Max helped by inventing likely minor assignments for me, and one of them I still remember. It was a wedding in a shabby street given over to second hand shops run by Polish Jews and patronized by sailors. The bride had written in demanding publicity, and I was sent to see her — partly as a means of gently hazing a freshman, but also on the chance that there might be a picturesque story in her. In the filthy shop downstairs her father directed me to the second floor, and when I climbed the stairs I found her in process of being dressed by her mother. She was standing in the middle of the floor with nothing on save a diaphanous vest and a flouncy pair of drawers. Never having seen a bride so close to the altogether before, I was somewhat upset, but she and her mother were quite calm, and loaded me with all the details of the impending ceremony. I wrote the story at length, but Max stuck it on his " If " hook, and there it died.

But such romantic interludes were not frequent. My days, like those of any other police reporter, were given over mainly to harsher matters — murders, assaults and batteries, street accidents, robberies, suicides, and so on. I well recall my first suicide, for the victim was a lovely young gal who had trusted a preacher's son too far, and then swallowed poison: she looked almost angelic lying on her parlor floor, with a couple of cops badgering her distracted mother. I remember, too, my first autopsy at the morgue — a most trying recreation for a hot Summer day —, and my first palaver with a burglar, and my first ride with the cops in a patrol-wagon, but for some reason or other my first murder has got itself forgotten. The young doctors at the City Hospital (now the Mercy Hospital) were always productive, for they did a heavy trade in street and factory accidents, and a very fair one in attempted suicides. In those days carbolic acid was the favorite drug among persons who yearned for the grave, just as bichloride of mercury was to be the favorite of a decade later, and I saw many of its customers brought in — their lips swollen horribly, and their eyes full of astonishment that they were still alive. Also, I saw people with their legs cut off, their arms torn off, their throats cut, their eyes gouged out. It was shocking for a little while, but then no more. Attached to the City Hospital was the first Pasteur Institute ever set up in America, and to it came patients from all over the South. It was in charge of an old doctor named Keirle, and usually he man-

aged to save them, but now and then one of them
reached him too late, and died of rabies in fright-
ful agony. He let me in on several of these death
scenes, with the poor patient strapped to the bed
and the nurses stepping warily. When the horror
became unendurable the old doctor would take over
with his hypodermic. He was a humane and ad-
mirable man, one of the few actual altruists that I
have ever known, and I marvel that the Baltimore
which has monuments to the founder of the Odd
Fellows and to the president of a third-rate railroad has never thought to honor itself by erecting
one to his memory.

On July 28, 1899, when I was precisely eighteen
years, ten months and sixteen days old, I saw my
first hanging; more, it was a hanging of the very
first chop, for no less than four poor blackamoors
were stretched at once. When I was assigned to it
as legman for one of the older reporters I naturally
suffered certain unpleasant forebodings, but the
performance itself did not shake me, though one of
the condemned lost his black cap in going through
the trap, and the contortions of his face made a
dreadful spectacle. The affair was staged in the
yard of the city jail, and there was a large gather-
ing of journalists, some of them from other cities,
for quadruple hangings, then as now, were fancy
goods. I went through the big iron gate at 5 a.m.,
and found that at least a dozen colleagues had been
on watch all night. Some of them had sustained

themselves with drafts from a bottle, and were already wobbling. When, after hours of howling by relays of colored evangelists, the four candidates were taken out and hanged, two of these bibbers and six or eight other spectators fell in swoons, and had to be evacuated by the cops. The sheriff of Baltimore was required by law to spring the trap, and he had prepared himself for that office by resorting to a bottle of his own. When it was performed he was assisted out of the jail yard by his deputies, and departed at once for Atlantic City, where he dug in for a week of nightmare.

I saw a good many hangings after that, some in Baltimore and the rest in the counties of Maryland. The county sheriffs always took aboard so much liquor for the occasion that they were virtually helpless: they could, with some help, pull the trap, but they were quite unable to tie the knot, bind the candidate, or carry off the other offices of the occasion. These were commonly delegated to Joe Heine, a gloomy German who had been chief deputy sheriff in Baltimore for many years, and was such a master of all the technics of his post that no political upheaval could touch him. So far as I know, Joe never actually put a man to death in his life, for that was the duty of the sheriff, but he traveled the counties tying knots and making the condemned ready, and there was never a slip when he officiated. I missed the great day of his career, which fell in 1904 or thereabout, for I was becoming bored with hangings by that time, and when a nearby county sheriff invited me to one as his private guest and well-wisher, I gave my ticket to my brother Charlie. This was Charlie's first experience and he saw a swell show indeed, for the candidate, a colored giant, fought Joe and the sheriff on the scaffold, knocked out the county cops who came to their aid, leaped down into the bellowing crowd, broke out of the jail yard, and took to an adjacent forest. It was an hour or more before he was run down and brought back. By that time all the fight had oozed out of him, and Joe and the sheriff turned him off with quiet elegance.

But a reporter chiefly remembers, not such routine themes of his art as hangings, fires and murders, which come along with dispiriting monotony, but the unprecedented novelties that occasionally inspire him, some of them gorgeous and others only odd. Perhaps the most interesting story I covered in my first six months had to do with the purloining of a cadaver from a medical college. The burglar was the head *Diener* of the dissecting-room, and he packed the body in a barrel and shipped it to a colleague in the upper Middle West, where there was a shortage of such provisions at the time. Hot weather coming on *en route*, it was discovered, and for a week we had a gaudy murder mystery. When the *Diener* shut off the uproar by confessing, it turned out that the maximum punishment he could be given, under the existing Maryland law, passed in 1730, was sixty days in the House of Correction. On his return to duty the medical students welcomed him with a beer party that lasted forty-eight hours, and he boasted that he had been stealing and shipping bodies for years. But the cops, discouraged, did nothing about it.

At a somewhat later time, after I had forsaken police reporting, the moral inadequacy of the ancient Maryland statutes was revealed again. This time the culprit was a Methodist clergyman who operated one of the vice crusades that then afflicted all the big cities of the East. The cops, of course, were violently against him, for they could see nothing wrong about honest women making honest livings according to their talents. When the pastor charged that they pooh-poohed him because they were taking bribes from the girls they determined to get him, and to that end sneaked a spy into the Y.M.C.A. One night soon afterward the pastor visited the place with a Christian young man, and the spy, concealed in a cupboard, caught the two in levantine deviltries. The former was collared at once, and the State's attorney sent for. Unhappily, he had to advise the poor cops that the acts they laid to their prisoner were not forbidden by Maryland law, which was singularly tolerant in sexual matters. The maximum penalty it then provided for adultery, however brutal and deliberate, was $10 fine, with no alternative of imprisonment, and there was no punishment at all for fornication, or for any of its non-Euclidian variations. The cops were thus stumped, but they quickly resolved their dilemma by concealing it from the scared pastor, and giving him two hours to get out of town. He departed leaving a wife and five children behind him, and has never been heard from since. The Legislature being in session, the cops then went to Annapolis and begged it to sharpen the laws. It responded by forbidding, under heavy penalties, a list of offenses so long and so bizarre that some of them are not even recorded in Krafft-Ebing.

I myself, while still assigned to the Central district, covered a case that well illustrated the humanity of the old Maryland statute. The accused was a man who had run away from Pittsburgh with another man's wife, and they had come to Baltimore in the drawing-room of a sleeper. The lady's husband, having got wind of their flight, wired ahead, asking the cops to arrest the pair on their arrival. The cops refused to collar an apparently respectable female on any such charge, but they brought in the man, and he was arraigned before Gene Grannan. As a matter of law, his guilt had to be presumed, for the Court of Appeals of Maryland had decided only a little while before that when a man and a woman went into a room together and locked the door it would be insane to give them the benefit of the doubt. Moreover, the prisoner, advised by a learned police-station lawyer, admitted the charge freely, and confined his defense to swearing that the crime had not been committed until after the train crossed the Maryland line. If he were sent back to Pennsylvania for trial he would be in serious difficulties, for the penalty for adultery there was almost as drastic as that for arson or piracy, but in Maryland, as I have said, it was a mere misdemeanor, comparable to breaking a window or spitting on the sidewalk. Grannan doubted the truth of the defense, but decided that a humane judge would have to accept it, so he fined the culprit $2, and the pair resumed their honeymoon with loud hosannas. When a Pennsylvania cop showed up the next day with extradition papers he was baffled, for the man had been tried and punished, and could not be put in jeopardy again.

Grannan held a session of his court every afternoon, and I always attended it. It was seldom, indeed, that he did not turn up something that made good copy. He had been, before his judicial days, chief of the Baltimore & Ohio's railroad police, and thus had a wide acquaintance among professional criminals, especially yeggmen, and held the professional respect of the cops. In that remote era there was no file of finger-prints at Washington, and even the Bertillon system was just coming into use. The cops, in consequence, sometimes picked up an eminent felon without knowing who he was. But if he came before Grannan he was identified at once, and started through a mill that commonly landed him in the Maryland Penitentiary. That institution, which occupied a fine new building near the city jail, then had as its warden a reformed politician named John Weyler. He had been a tough baby in his day, and was even suspected of a hand in a homicide, but when I knew him he had said goodbye to all that, and was an excellent officer. I dropped in on him two or three times a week, and usually picked up something worth printing. He had a strange peculiarity: he never came outside the prison walls save when it was raining. Then he would wander around for hours, and get himself soaked to the skin, for he never used an umbrella. Once a month his board of visitors met at the Penitentiary, and he entertained the members at dinner. These dinners gradually took on lavishness and gaiety, and during one of them a member of the board, searching for a place marked " Gents," fell down the main staircase of the place and had to be sent to hospital. After that Weyler limited the drinks to ten or twelve a head.

Another good source of the kind of news that Max Ways liked was an old fellow named Hackman, the superintendent of the morgue. The morgue was housed in an ancient building at the end of one of the city docks, and Hackman seldom left it. There was a sort of derrick overhanging the water, and on it the harbor cops would pull up the floaters that they found, and let them dry. Some of them were covered with crabs and barnacles when they were brought in, and Hackman had a long pole for knocking such ornaments off. How greatly he loved his vocation was shown when a new health commissioner fired him, and he refused to give up his keys. The health commissioner thereupon called for a squad of cops, and went down to the morgue to take possession by force, followed by a trail of reporters. But Hackman was defiant, and when firemen were sent for to aid the cops, he barricaded himself among his clients, and declared that he would never be taken alive.

The ensuing battle went on all afternoon, and was full of thrills. The cops refused to resort to firearms and the firemen refused to knock down the door with their hose, so Hackman seemed destined to hold out forever. Every now and then he would open the door for a few inches, and howl fresh defiance at the health commissioner. Finally, one of the reporters, Frank R. Kent, of the *Sun*, sneaked up along the wall, and thrust in his foot the next time the door was opened. Before Hackman could hack Kent's foot off the cops rushed him, and the morgue was taken. The poor old fellow burst into tears as he was being led away. The morgue, he wailed, was his only solace, almost his only life; he had devoted years to its upkeep and improvement, and was proud of its high standing among the morgues of Christendom. Moreover, many of the sponges, cloths and other furnishings within, including the pole he used to delouse floaters, were his personal property, and he was being robbed of them. The health commissioner promised to restore them, and so Hackman faded from the scene, a victim to a Philistine society that could not fathom his peculiar ideals.

There were press-agents in those days as in these, and though they had not reached the dizzy virtuosity now on tap they nevertheless showed a considerable ingenuity and daring. One of the best I encountered in my first years remains unhappily nameless in my memory, though I well recall some of his feats. He slaved for Frank Bostock, a big, blond, tweedy, John Bullish Englishman who had leased an old cyclorama in Baltimore and put in a wild animal show. Even before the doors were open the agent bombarded the local newspapers with bulletins worthy the best tradition of Tody Hamilton, press-agent for P. T. Barnum — battles between tigers and boa constrictors, the birth of infant giraffes and kangaroos, the sayings of a baboon who could speak Swahili, and so on. When, after the opening, business turned out to be bad, he spit on his hands, and turned off some masterpieces. The one I remember best was the hanging of a rogue elephant, for I was assigned to cover it. This elephant, we were informed, had become so onery that he could be endured no longer, and it was necessary to put him to death. Ordinarily, he would be shot, but Bostock, as a patriotic and law-abiding Englishman, preferred hanging, and would serve as executioner himself.

The butchery of the poor beast — he looked very mangey and feeble — was carried out one morning in the Bolton street railroad yards. First his legs were tied together, and then a thick hawser was passed around his neck and pulled tight, and the two ends were fastened to the hook of a railroad crane. When Bostock gave the signal the crane began to grind, and in a few minutes the elephant was in the air. He took it very quietly, and was pronounced dead in half an hour. A large crowd saw the ceremony, and after that business at the Bostock zoo picked up. The press-agent got rid of the S.P.C.A. by announcing that the elephant had been given six ounces of morphine to dull his sensations. His remains were presented to the Johns Hopkins Medical School for scientific study, but no one there was interested in proboscidean anatomy, so they finally reached a glue factory.

Six months later the Bostock zoo gave the Baltimore newspapers a good story without any effort by its press-agent. On a cold Winter night, with six inches of sleet in the streets, it took fire, and in a few minutes all its major inmates were burned to death and the small fry were at large. The pursuit of the latter went on all night and all the next day, and the cops turned up an occasional frost-bitten monkey as much as a week later. No really dangerous animal got loose, but the town was in a state of terror for weeks, and many suburban dogs, mistaken for lions or tigers, were done to death by vigilantes. I recall picking up a powerful cold by wallowing around the night of the fire in the icy slush.

But the best of all the Baltimore press-agents of that age was a volunteer who worked for the sheer love of the science. His name was Frank Thomas, and he was the son of a contractor engaged in building a new courthouse. There were to be ten or twelve huge marble pillars in the façade of the building, and they had to be brought in from a quarry at Cockeysville, fourteen miles away. The hauling was done on trucks drawn by twenty horses. One day a truck lost a wheel and the pillar aboard was broken across the middle. Frank announced at once that a fossil dog had been found in the fracture, and supported the tale by having a crude dog painted on it and the whole photographed. That photograph made both the *Herald* and the *American*, though the suspicious *Sunpaper* sniffed at it. It took the geologists at the Johns Hopkins a week to convince the town that there could be no canine fossils in sedimentary rocks. A bit later Frank made it known that the new courthouse would be fitted with a contraption that would suck up all sounds coming in from the streets, and funnel them out through the sewers. In his handout he described eloquently the comfort of judges

and juries protected against the noises of traffic
and trade, and the dreadful roar of the accumulated sounds as they emerged from the sewers along
the waterfront. Frank indulged himself in many
other inventions, and I handled most of them for
the *Herald*, for the courthouse was in my parish.
When the building was finished at last he published an illustrated souvenir book on it, and I
wrote the 8000 words of its text. My honorarium
was $25.

His days, alas, were not all beer and skittles, for
putting up a large building in the heart of a busy
city is a job shot through with cephalalgia. While
it was under way a high board fence surrounded it,
and on that fence were all the usual advertising
signs, most of them hideous. The *Herald* started a
violent crusade against them, arguing that they
disgraced the courthouse and affronted all decent
people. I was assigned by Max Ways to write some
of the indignant stories we printed, and thus I met
Frank in the dual rôle of friend of his fancy and
enemy of his fence. So far as I could make out, the
Herald's crusade had no support whatsoever in
public sentiment — in fact, it became more and
more difficult to find anyone to endorse it — but
it roared on for months. The fence came down at
last at least three or four weeks later than it would
have come down if there had been no hullabaloo,
for Frank had iron in him as well as imagination,
and held out defiantly as long as he could.

It was a crusading time, with uplifters of a hundred schools harrying every major American city, and every newspaper of any pretensions took a hand in the dismal game. I recall crusades against sweat-shops, against the shanghaiing of men for the Chesapeake oyster fleet, and against dance-halls that paid their female interns commissions on the drinks sold. I had a hand in all of them, and if they filled me with doubts they also gave me some exhilarating experiences. With the cops I toured the bastiles of the waterfront crimps, and examined the jails that they maintained for storing their poor bums, and with health department inspectors I saw all the worst sweat-shops of the town, including one in which a huge flock of hens was kept hard at work laying eggs in a filthy cellar. In the war upon bawdy dance-halls I became a witness, unwillingly, against the cops, for I was put on the stand to testify that I had seen two detectives in one of them, and that the detectives must have been aware of what was going on. The poor flatfeet were unquestionably guilty, for I had discussed the matter with them in the place, but I managed to sophisticate my testimony with so many ifs and buts that it went for nothing, and they were acquitted by the police board. That was my first and last experience as an active agent of moral endeavor. I made up my mind at once that my true and natural allegiance was to the Devil's party, and it has been my firm belief ever since that all persons who devote themselves to forcing virtue on their fellow men deserve nothing better than kicks in the pants. Years later I put that belief into a proposition which I ventured to call Mencken's Law, to wit:

Whenever A annoys or injures B on the pretense of saving or improving X, A is a scoundrel.

The moral theologians, unhappily, have paid no heed to this contribution to their science, and so Mencken's Law must wait for recognition until the dawn of a more enlightened age.

SERGEANT'S STRIPES

WHEN I project my mind back into space and time it gathers in more pictures from my days as a police reporter than from any other period, and they have more color in them, and a keener sense of delight. But they were actually not long, for before I had been on the *Herald* staff a year I was promoted out of the world of common or dirt felony and assigned to cover the more subtle skullduggeries of the City Hall. This promotion was surely not to be sniffed at, for the City Hall assignment was then regarded by all reporters as something choice and important, and is so regarded, in fact, to this day. Moreover, it gave me more chance to shine than I had had in police work, and so got me frequent offers from the other Baltimore papers, and jacked up my salary on the *Herald*. I find by an old account-book that my first raise from $7 to $8 a week was not lifted to $10 until the beginning of 1900, but during the ensuing Summer I was promoted to $14, in December to $16, and in February, 1901, to $18. But during my first weeks in the City Hall I was homesick for Gene Grannan and the cops, the jail and the morgue. I was still very green — indeed, much greener than I was aware of in my youthful vanity — and it took me some time to fathom the art of handling politicians. Even the ordinary routine of City Hall reporting was full of snares, and I fell into some of them.

One fetched me on my very first day in the new service. There had been a municipal election during the previous Spring, and though its results were long known and its victors in office, the official returns had not yet been published by the Board of Election Supervisors. They were now, it appeared, to be given to a waiting world. Unhappily, I was slowed down in my tour of the City Hall by my unfamiliarity with its very geography, and when I got to the office of the supervisors at last it was closed for the day. I can still remember every twinge of my terror. What if I fell down on the story? The least penalty I could imagine would be return to a police assignment — and maybe not even a good one. So I hopped a trolley-car and tracked down the secretary to the board — an amiable politico whose name was Deane. He was sitting down to supper, but I conveyed to him enough of my alarm to induce him to come down to his office at once, open his safe, and give me a copy of the returns. When I got to the *Herald* office late, and Max Ways froze me with a growl, I thought it best to tell him the truth. He received it with a tolerant smile. " If you were older," he said, " you'd have known better. Such official documents are not worth so much trouble. If you had come in without it I could have got a proof of it from Jim Doyle [city editor of the *American*] or Hallett [city editor of the *Sun*]. But don't think that I blame you. We live and learn."

My relief was stupendous, and I chalked up one more article in my long bill of debts to Max. Soon afterward he quit the *Herald* and newspaper work, and was succeeded by a new city editor who had been, only lately, a City Hall reporter himself, so I had to hustle, and hustle I did. My job was gradually made pleasant, though surely not lightened, by the fact that the Mayor then in office — he had come in but a short time before — was an extremely eccentric and rambunctious fellow, so full of surprises that he had already acquired the nickname of Thomas the Sudden. His name was Hayes, and he was at one and the same time a very shrewd lawyer, an unconstructed Confederate veteran, a pious Methodist, and a somewhat bawdy bachelor. He was a wiry little fellow with a high forehead and a gigantic black moustache, and was the precise image of the Nietzsche depicted in Hans Olde's familiar drawing. There never lived on this earth a more quarrelsome man. He never had less than

six feuds going at once, and some of them reached
unparalleled altitudes of raucousness. When he
could not fetch his enemies by any other method he
sued them in the courts, and during all of his four-
year term the appellate judges of Maryland were
kept humping by his litigations. There was in
Baltimore at the time another litigant of ferocious
assiduity, to wit, Charles J. Bonaparte, who was a
grand-nephew of Napoleon I and was later to become Secretary of the Navy and then Attorney
General in the Cabinet of Roosevelt I. But Bonaparte usually lost his cases, and in fact frittered
away on them the better part of an inherited fortune of $1,000,000, whereas Hayes invariably won.

His method of celebrating victory was to go on a
grand drunk. One evening, in the course of such a
drunk, he arrived home in a state of incoördination,
and fell down a stairway in his house, breaking a
leg. After that, for a couple of months, the City
Hall reporters of Baltimore had to see him in bed,
and loud and long were the snorts and screams of
moral indignation that issued from it. He lived
with his sister, an old maid schoolma'm, and she
tried her best to police him, but with very little success. Propped up in a frayed and filthy nightshirt,
he chewed tobacco all his waking hours, and spit
the juice into space without stopping to aim. On a
table beside his bed was a box of five-cent cigars,
but I never saw him smoke one, and he never offered
one to a visitor. It was his theory that his enemies

in and out of the City Hall were taking advantage of his disablement to ruin his administration, reduce Baltimore to bankruptcy, and undermine civilization, and in support of that theory he was always ready with great masses of evidence, some of it more or less plausible, but most of it plainly bogus. We reporters had to sift the little that could be printed from the mass that was poisonously libellous, and sometimes the job was anything but easy. But we liked the old boy nevertheless, for good stories radiated from him like quills from the fretful portentine, and if we had to scrap two-thirds of his fulminations there was always enough left to keep us rich in copy.

He was one of the most brazen boasters I have ever encountered, but I soon learned from him the immoral but useful lesson that boasters are not necessarily liars. He was, in fact, a really first-rate public official, and he pretty well cleaned out the corruption that had burdened Baltimore for generations, and set up so rational and efficient a municipal administration that its momentum is still visible, though he has been dead many years. His chief enemy, rather curiously, was another Confederate veteran whose honesty and competence were as notable as his own. This was Major Richard M. Venable, a member of the City Council and one of the stars of the Maryland bar. Though the two were on the same side at bottom, and both served Baltimore magnificently, they always differed in detail, and inasmuch as neither could ever imagine the slightest decency in an opponent, they carried on their wars *à outrance* and kept the town in a dither. Once they landed before the Court of Appeals at Annapolis on nine separate points of law, and though Venable was the more learned lawyer, and by far, Hayes won on every point. His celebration went on for weeks, and in the course of it he issued statements sneering at Venable as a putrid pettifogger, questioning the election returns that put him in the Council, and even hinting that there was something phony about his war record. None of them were ever printed.

Venable was also a bachelor, and a personage quite as picturesque as Hayes himself. He was of great stature, had a belly so vast that his waistcoat looked like a segment of balloon, and wore a huge and bristling beard. He kept house in a sort of one-man monastery in a decayed downtown street, and was beautifully served by a staff of colored servants. One dull Sunday evening, seeking only to set him to talking, I asked him how he managed to run his establishment so well. He replied that there were two reasons. The first was that no white women were allowed in the house, and the second was that he had a standing offer to his servants to pay them half again as much as anyone else was willing to pay them. He had two great hates, one against women and the other against Christianity.

His large library was principally made up of works on theology, and he read them constantly, and damned them violently. He was, in fact, the premier town atheist of his generation, and after his death it was reported that he had left orders that his ashes were to be disposed of by throwing them into any convenient ashcan. If he actually left such orders they were disregarded; instead, his ashes were scattered in Druid Hill Park, for in his last days he had been a member of the Park Board. His loathing of women embraced the whole sex, but its worst poisons were concentrated on a lady eminent in good works. It was a common joke in Baltimore city-rooms to send a new reporter to him for verification of a presumed report that he was about to marry her. His roars usually scared the reporter out of a month's growth.

The major easily dominated both houses of the City Council, and it usually served him docilely in his gory wars on Mayor Hayes. It consisted, then as always, of a scattering of intelligent raisins in a big loaf of dunderheads. One of its members was a brewery collector, another was a writer of dime novels, and two others were operators of O.E.A. (*i.e.*, odorless excavating apparatus) companies, which is to say, they were engaged professionally in cleaning the privies that survived in thousands of Baltimore backyards until 1915 or thereabout, when the sewerage system was completed. The rest sloped down to saloonkeepers, small trucking contractors, and miscellaneous ward-heelers. The major rode these poor idiots in a bold and berserk fashion, and whenever one of them ventured to vote against him, which was not often, he gave a magnificent exhibition of moral indignation. They trembled under his bellowing, but like inferior men at all times and everywhere, ended by admiring him vastly, and even, in their dull way, loving him. Sometimes he would gather them together in one of the council chambers after a meeting had adjourned, and delight them with Rabelaisian anecdotes in the manner of Abraham Lincoln. He had a large répertoire, and his delivery was aided considerably by his commanding mien and florid beard.

It was part of my job, of course, to cover the sessions of the Council, and I always enjoyed them greatly. Inasmuch as there were two houses I was given an assistant for the duration, but I usually managed to look in at both chambers, and never missed the upper one when Major Venable was on his legs. The hour of meeting was 5 p.m. and the sessions often lasted until 8. We reporters were allowed 50 cents a head by our papers for supper money, and usually victualled before returning to our offices, for in those primitive days the maniacal demand for early copy that now palsies journalism was unheard of. Across the street from the City Hall there was a saloon in which a dinner consisting of a coriaceous T-bone steak, a dab of fried

potatoes, a slice of rye bread and a cup of coffee
could be had for a quarter, and most of the reporters patronized it, and so made a profit of the
other quarter. But there was one among them of
more voluptuous inclinations, and he soon convinced me that it was better to eat a more elegant
dinner. He was Frank Kent, of the *Sun*. He had
discovered that such a meal was on tap in a hotel in
Calvert street, and thereafter he and I ate it every
Council night. Sometimes we had to add ten cents
to the fifty to cover our checks, but we were reck-
less fellows, and did not begrudge any kindness to
our pyloruses.

This epicureanism rather set us apart from the
other City Hall reporters, and our singularity was
even more unpleasantly marked when we gave
Major Venable aid and applause in his war upon
what had been known for years and years as " the
meritorious measure." This was an ordinance put
through whenever the Council adjourned for its
Summer recess, giving every reporter who had
covered its proceedings a gratuity of $150. It had
been passed yearly since the Civil War, and maybe
since the Revolution, but the major announced that
he was implacably agin it, and, what is more, that
he would attack it in a taxpayer's suit if it were
passed. Frank and I, having convinced ourselves
virtuously that any such gratuity was an insult to
journalism, let it be known that we'd refuse the
money if the major came to grief, and this got us

some unpopularity among our colleagues, but when he won hands down the matter was quickly forgotten, and we were again on good terms with all hands. There were so many sources of news in the City Hall that it was impossible for one reporter to cover all of them, so we had perforce to pool our daily accumulations. How that arrangement once broke down, and how human ingenuity restored it, will be told in Chapter XVIII.

The examples of Hayes and Venable were proofs enough that honest and competent men could sometimes get on the public payroll, and I soon found many more on lower levels. Hayes's secretary, a courtly Irishman named William A. Ryan, was one, and another was a man named Julius Freeman, who was deputy city register: both knew their jobs and gave the city hard and faithful service. A third was a curious character named McCuen, a bachelor like Hayes and Venable, and like Venable again, the master of a fierce set of whiskers. McCuen's were almost as red as blood, and he wore them parted in the middle, and drawn out into two horns. He came from South Baltimore, and his past was that of any other neighborhood politico, but when Hayes made him superintendent of lamps and lighting he took his duties with great gravity, and was soon discharging them in a highly efficient and even stylish manner. All day he slaved in his office, and half the night he roved the streets, spotting lights that were not working, and picking out

places to set up new ones. For the first time in its
history Baltimore was decently lighted. Moreover,
McCuen replaced thousands of the old rickety
lamp-posts with new ones of excellent design, and
in general showed an aesthetic sense that was astounding in a politician. But now and then he reverted unaccountably to more primitive canons of
taste, and once he spent a lot of money putting
colored lights into a fountain in one of the city
reservoirs. The effect was that of an explosion of
stick-candy, but more Baltimoreans admired it
than laughed at it, and the lights remain in place
to this day, forty years afterward.

At about the same time a Civil War veteran who
was superintendent of the City Hall decided that
the large bronze lamps which flanked its main entrance were too dirty to be endured, and had his
men give them a coat of bright green paint. This
improvement set loose an uproar, for the patina on
them had been accumulating for thirty years, and
was much prized by the town cognoscenti. I well
recall the distress of the poor old man when he
finally took in the notion that his honest effort to
imitate the arty McCuen had resulted in a *faux
pas*. I really felt sorry for him, but my responsibility to my own art had to be considered first, so I
helped to heap ribaldry upon him. The Baltimore
cartoonists had a grand time while his agony lasted.
McKee Barclay of the *Evening News* did a plate
showing all the principal local monuments be-

dizened in the new manner, including the Washington column striped like a barber's pole. It took the City Hall scavengers two weeks to scrape the paint off the lamps, and in doing so they removed the patina too.

The City Hall seemed dullish after the Central police district, but even so it had its moments. There was a battle in the war between Hayes and Venable every few weeks, and in the intervals the members of the various city boards locked horns, and gave us good shows. During the Winter smallpox broke out in Baltimore, and patients dragged out of the alleys by the cops were stored every afternoon in the City Hall annex, an old school building occupied by the Health Department, a block or so away from the Hall itself. Whenever a wagonload accumulated it was started for the pesthouse down the harbor. Visiting the Health Department every day, we reporters had to pass within a few feet of these candidates for the potter's field. To protect us the doctors vaccinated us once a week. The vaccinations produced less effect on me than so many gnat bites, for my arm had been scraped back in 1882 by our family physician, Dr. Z. K. Wiley, and when he did a job of that kind he left behind him a scar like a shell crater, good for a generation.

Hayes distrusted all his official advisers, and especially his legal staff, but he had a kitchen cabinet that had his confidence, composed mainly of

third-rate politicians. One Sunday I printed in the
Herald what purported to be a report of its latest
star-chamber proceedings, and the buffoonery was
so well received that I went on with it thereafter
from week to week. In a little while one of the members offered to give me more or less accurate minutes of its actual sessions if I would agree to treat
him politely. I agreed readily, and after that my
stories were accepted in the City Hall as authentic.
Hayes himself tried to worm out of me the source
of my information, but the pieces were unsigned,
and I refused to admit that I was writing them.
His suspicions were finally fixed on a quite innocent
member, and this unfortunate was expelled from
the cabinet, and threatened with the loss of his city
job. It is a remarkable fact that the member who
really leaked was never detected, and indeed never
even suspected. I kept on writing this somewhat
obvious stuff until my term of servitude in the City
Hall ended. Even today I occasionally meet an old-
time politician who remembers it uneasily, and tries
to induce me to tell him who blabbed. More than
once my report of the cabinet's debates, touched up
artistically, ruined some design of Hayes and his
torpedoes, and covered Major Venable with sooth-
ing unguents. But the major never admitted that
he read such trivia. He was essentially a serious
man.

Hayes himself came to a bad end. After his four-
years' term as Mayor he dropped out of politics,

and resumed his law practise, which was mainly devoted to criminal business. He knew how to holler in court and was thus successful before juries, but in Maryland most criminal trials go on without juries, even in capital cases, and he made much less impression on judges. A Methodist by early training, he gradually gave over the jug and devoted himself more and more to Christian endeavor. He became the superintendent of a Methodist Sunday-school, and inveigled the *Sunday Sun* into printing his weekly observations on the International Sunday-school Lessons. These observations were of a high degree of fatuity, and when I became Sunday editor of the *Sun* myself, in 1906, I killed them. In his last years, which were lonely and unhappy, for his schoolma'm sister had died, his income was diminishing and his services to Baltimore were beginning to be forgotten, he wasted at least half his time on his theological debauchery, greatly to the distress of his former secretary, Ryan, who was a very intelligent man, and moreover, a Catholic. Ryan himself had made progress in politics, and was by now collector of customs. I dropped in on him often, and we moaned over poor Hayes's deterioration, but there was nothing that we could do about it. When he died at last his funeral orgies were on a scale fit for a bishop, or even an archangel, and the Methodists of Baltimore still remember him as a prophet comparable to Nehemiah, Habakkuk or Deuteronomy. But to all the less sanctified Baltimoreans he has grown vague, and there is no public memorial to him in the town.

He was the last of the Civil War veterans to reach high public office there, and even during his term as Mayor the old city was changing. The great fire of 1904 was to hasten its transmogrification, and today it bears little resemblance to the Baltimore of my first memories. But in my reportorial days there were still whole sections, especially along the waterfront, that still looked and smelled exactly as they must have looked and smelled in 1861. The Back Basin, which made up into the town so far that its head was only four blocks from the main crossroads, received the effluence of such sewers as existed, and emitted a stench as cadaverous and unearthly as that of the canals of Venice. In Summer it took on extra voltage, and became almost unendurable, but the old-time Baltimoreans pretended that they didn't notice it, and even professed to believe that it was good for their sinuses and a prophylactic against the ague. During the crusading era the local newspapers often set up demands that something be done about it, but it continued to afflict the town until the new sewerage system was completed, and the Back Basin was reduced to the humble status of a receptacle for rain water. Once a *Herald* editorial writer proposed in print, and quite seriously, that a dam be built across the mouth of the Basin, to the end that the water backed up at high tide might be released suddenly when the tide was low. His theory was that the resultant flood would carry off all the dead dogs, decayed bunches of bananas and multitudinous worse filth that floated on the Basin's surface. When an Old Subscriber wrote in asking what would happen to the shipping in the lower harbor when this flood roared down the Patapsco, the editorial writer was indignant, and accused various reporters of writing the letter.

My days in the City Hall, like my days as a police reporter, were not long, but by the time they were over I had begun to think of myself as a journeyman journalist, and was so accepted by the elder brethren of the craft. It was not unusual for me to be taken off the job for a day or two, or even for a week or two, and assigned to some other work. After the middle of 1900 I had a hand in nearly all the big stories that engaged the Baltimore newspapers. Even in 1899 I had been told off to do the election-day lead, and given three columns for it. It was a story of some importance, for up to that time Baltimore had never seen an election day without at least one murder. But the tide was now flowing toward peace and decorum, and though I roved the town all day, looking for dead and wounded, I had to base my lead on the surprising fact that no one had been killed, and only a few poor bums hurt. The next year I was put to writing a pre-election series of instructions to voters, for the election laws had been lately changed by taking all party emblems off the ballots, which thus became Chinese puzzles to the plain people, who had been voting for either Abraham Lincoln's beard or the Democratic rooster for years. At the time I performed this educational service I had just passed my twentieth birthday, and could not vote myself until nearly a year later.

I was used to newspaper hours by now, and liked them. On Summer nights it was always beginning to grow cool when I got home — sometimes as early as one o'clock, but usually nearer three. I got in some reading in the quiet of the house, and slept like a top. Arising at ten or thereabouts, I had a couple of hours for my literary enterprises before going to work. I lost a good many days off, but those that I got were very pleasant, for they gave me some extra time for writing, and in the evening I went to the theatre. As older men dropped out I inherited Saturday as my day off — the choice one of the whole week, for there were matinées on it, and some sort of newspaper party was always staged after work on Saturday night. I began to reflect upon my trade, and to discern some of its principal virtues and defects. Of the latter, the worst was the fact that it worked me too hard, but though I was aware of it I did not resent it, for I was still full of the eagerness of youth, and hot to see the whole show. Of the former, the greatest was that a newspaper man always saw that show from a reserved seat in the first row. The rest of humanity had to wait in line and struggle for places, but not a reporter. He was always expected, and usually welcomed. He got into places by a side door. To this day it always irritates me absurdly to have to stand in line, even for a few minutes — say at a ticket-window or on a customs pier. It seems to me to be an intolerable affront, not only to my private pomp and circumstance, but also to the honor of the Fourth Estate.

IV

APPROACH TO

LOVELY LETTERS

Wʜᴇɴ I told Max Ways, on applying for a job on the *Herald*, that I had been busting with literary ardors for four or five years I was stating a simple fact. It must have been before 1895 that I made my first formal attempt to do something for publication: it was an article on a chemical invention of my own — a platinum toning bath for silver photographic prints. All the photographic magazines of the time rejected it, and it never got into print until 1925, when the late Isaac Goldberg published it in a book called " The Man Mencken." I was in those days vacillating between chemistry and journalism, and two teachers at the Baltimore Polytechnic, from which I was graduated in 1896 as the youngest member of my class, had something to do with my final choice. I had got interested in chemistry through photography, and in photography through the gift of a camera at Christmas, 1892, just as I had got interested in journalism through the gift of a printing-press at Christmas, 1888.

By 1894 I had a laboratory in Hollins street, and was engaged in eager but usually inconclusive experiments. All the orthodox accidents happened to me, including four or five explosions and an inhalation of bromide gas that nearly strangled me, and no doubt had something to do with the sore throat that pestered me for years afterward. If I had encountered a competent teacher of chemistry at the Polytechnic I'd have gone on in that science, and today I'd be up to my ears in the vitamines, for it was synthetic chemistry that always interested me most. But the gogue told off to nurture me succeeded only in disheartening me, so I gradually edged over to letters, helped by another gogue who really knew his stuff, and, what is more, loved it. He was a young *Cand. jur.* named Edward S. Kines, who had but recently graduated from the Baltimore City College, and was pursuing his legal studies of an evening at the University of Maryland Law School. He taught English literature at the Polytechnic, and judged by any plausible standard must have been set down a bad teacher, but somehow or other he managed to impart to me, and to a few other boys, his honest enthusiasm for what then passed in schools for good books. My reading, up to the time he began to operate on me, had been scattered and futile, but he gave it direction, and I was soon leaping and prancing through the whole classical répertoire, and enjoying it. I even tackled such revolting doses as Butler's " Hudibras," Herbert's " The Temple," the contributions to the *Spectator* by Eustace Budgell, and Colley Cibber's Apology.

Kines, so far as I know, had no literary ambitions of his own: he was content to spout his favorite passages, and in his later years he devoted himself assiduously to his trade as a trial lawyer. Nor was there much scratching for the *cacoethes scribendi* among his pupils. Indeed, I can recall but one who ever spoke of writing. He was Arthur W. Hawks, who had a brother on the *Herald* staff, and was to join it himself a little while before I did. It may be that the example of the two Hawkses led me to the *Herald* instead of to the *Sun*, but on that point my memory is cloudy, and I am sure that they knew little about my actual attempts at writing, at any rate before 1898. I recall going out to the Baltimore baseball grounds in 1895, and doing a play-by-play report of a game between the famous Baltimore Orioles and some visiting nine, but though I was delighted the next morning to find that it coincided with the stories in the newspapers I never showed it to anyone. Nor did I solicit opinion on any of the verse that I began to do about the same time. Indeed, I have always been shy about showing my writings to other people, though it would certainly be an exaggeration to call me, generally speaking, a violet; and to this day I have never asked anyone to read a manuscript of mine, or even a printed book. My first production was a satirical poem on a baseball theme, and I sent it to the Baltimore *American* unsigned, and was amazed to see it in print. After that I favored the *American* with almost daily contributions, but only one more was ever printed. At the Polytechnic my yearning to make the staff of the school paper was thwarted by the class politicians, and when the time came to concoct a class play I was not invited to help write it, but put to banging the piano for the performance.

To a youngster of my inclinations the literary movement of the nineties was naturally a cosmic event, and I followed it as best I could, with no one to guide me, once I had departed from Kines. I remember haunting a newsdealer's shop in West Baltimore, hot to grab every new magazine as it came out, and first and last I must have waded through scores of them. The majority were idiotically eccentric: there was one, for example, in which the illustrations, printed separately, were pasted in, and another that sold pretentiously for a cent. But my critical faculties were still embryonic, and I devoured the bad with the good. The *Chap-Book* and the *Lark* went through my mill, but so did

many an arty monstrosity that lasted but one number. I recall, however, enjoying *M'lle New York*
better than most, for there was in it a writer named
James G. Huneker whose illuminating sophistica-
tion and colorful, rapid style gave me a special
thrill. Years later I was to know him well and see
much of him, but in 1895 he was as far out of my
world as Betelgeuse.

When I began to find my way about the *Herald*
office I discovered to my delight that I was on the
actual frontiers of lovely letters, for all those members of the staff who showed a mental age above
thirteen were consumed by either one or the other
of two then prevalent ambitions: to write the book
of a comic opera, or to set up a weekly journal of
literary, theatrical, musical and political opinion.
The elder Hawks, Wells, was actually engaged
upon the former, and though, as a young reporter,
I was not admitted to his confidences, his brother
Arthur sneaked some of its lyrics to show me, and
we agreed that they were masterpieces. No weekly
ever precipitated itself from the current dreams,
but a monthly called *Dixie* was really in existence,
and if the contributions of the local literati made
no noise, the magazine was at least getting notice
for some of its illustrations. They were done by a
pen-and-ink artist named G. Alden Peirson. Turning away from the uptown prides and glories of
Baltimore, he went down to the waterfront for his
subjects, and there produced some very charming

drawings.[1] The newspaper artists of the town were naturally miles behind him, but they, too, had their quest for an earthly Grail. It took them to a dark office in an old building under the elevated in North street, where there lurked a syndicate man who was always ready to buy a comic drawing of the sort then in fashion. Unhappily, there had to be a he-and-she joke to go with it, and inventing these jokes usually stumped the artists. When they could not find a literary reporter able to supply one, they went to the Pratt Library and dug it out of the back files of *Puck*, *Judge* or *Texas Siftings*. The market price for joke and drawing was $1.

There were some high-toned literati living in Baltimore in those days — for example, Edward Abram Uffington Valentine, who printed a book of poems in 1902 that got very good reviews — but I never met any of them, and there was little to lift me, after I got used to it, in the endless gabble that went on in the *Herald* office about the weekly that never came to birth. My own aspirations were gradually turning from poetry to prose. I had a drawer full of verse, but I was making fewer and fewer additions to it. A large part of it consisted of dreadful imitations of Kipling, who was then my god, and the rest was made up of triolets, rondeaux and other experiments in the old French forms that

---

[1] *Dixie* lasted from January, 1899, to April, 1900. The rest of its illustrations scarcely got above the candy-box-top level. Its literary contents were even worse.

Austin Dobson and Andrew Lang had brought in. In the Autumn of 1900, when I was given a weekly column on the editorial page, and invited to do my damnedest, I unearthed a lot of these *Jugendwerke,* and so saved the labor of writing new stuff. They were all pretty bad, but they seemed to be well received in the office, and in December I received the singular honor of being invited by the new managing editor, Carter, to do a poem for the first page. It was not, to be sure, quite original, for it was based upon a French piece lately published by Edmond Rostand, roundly denouncing the Boer leader, Oom Paul Kruger. Carter put Rostand's French into English prose, and I turned it into burning tetrameter, with poor old Oom reduced to a greasepot at the end. It was blowsy stuff, God knows, but Carter professed to like it, and, good or bad, there it glowed and glittered in long primer italic on page one — a glory that no other American poet, however gifted, has ever achieved, at least to my knowledge. My column ran on until my reserves of prosody began to be depleted. I then diluted it with more and more prose, and finally it became prose altogether. Beginning in June, 1901, it took the form of a weekly tale of ancient Rome, in which all the characters were American politicians, thinly disguised. Every tale ended with the hanging of the principal personage. I don't recall how many such pieces I did, but it was well beyond thirty, and toward the end of the series I was hard put to invent something new every week, and yet keep within the formula.

My poetical contributions to the editorial page in 1900 and 1901 made up most of the contents of my first book, " Ventures Into Verse," though it did not come out until 1903. It was a typical product of the aesthetic movement of the time, then gradually subsiding. Its projectors were two young fellows named Marshall and Beek, who had formed a firm to do fine printing and taken into partnership an artist named Gordon. The three came to me asking that I suggest a likely source of copy for a small volume that would show off their advanced typography, and I naturally nominated myself. Marshall set the book by hand, and there were decorations by Gordon, and by another artist named John Siegel. The press-run was 100 copies, of which I got half and the firm got half. Some were bound à la Roycroft, in rough binders' boards with red labels, but most were issued in plain brown paper. I sent ten of my copies to the principal critical organs of the time, and presented the rest to libraries or to friends. As incredible as it may seem, the book got good notices, but only three orders for it ever reached Marshall, Beek and Gordon. My presentation copies seem to have been preserved in odd corners, for when American firsts began to bring fantastic prices, in 1925, a good many appeared in the market, and at one time a clean specimen brought as much as $225. All those that had gone to public libraries were stolen. Some ass spread the story that I was buying up the copies offered by dealers, and burning them. It was, of course, not true. I can recall buying but one copy, and that one I gave to a friend. It cost me $130.

Meanwhile, I was devoting all my meagre leisure to writing. I still did an occasional poem, and some of them were published in magazines. The first to make high literary society, so far as I can recall, was a rhymed address to my hero Kipling, urging him to forget politics and go back to Mandalay. It was written in the Autumn of 1899, while I was in the midst of my apprenticeship as a police reporter, and I sent it to the *Bookman*, then edited by Harry Thurston Peck. It went in anonymously and with no return address on the manuscript, and I was both surprised and enchanted when it came out in the December issue. I wrote to Peck at once, admitting its paternity with suitable blushes, and was surprised again when one of his assistants replied politely, and enclosed a check for $10. I quote from the letter:

As we are paying you more than we usually do for poems, you may judge from that fact that the poem appealed to us. We may add, also, that the poem has been quoted quite a little in the newspapers.

I recall a curious detail of the day the December *Bookman* appeared on the newsstands in Baltimore.

When I discovered my verses in it I was so addled that I was quite unfit for work, and decided to seek peace and recuperation in the old Odeon Theatre in Frederick street, to which I had the entrée. The Odeon was a burlesque house, and while I sat in a stage box, reading my burning lines over and over again, two comedians broke slapsticks over each other's fundaments, and the ladies of the ensemble engaged in what were then called muscle dances. But the manager of the house, James Madison, was himself a writer,[2] and when he dropped in on me and I showed him the magazine he joined in my rejoicings. On returning to the *Herald* office, I told Max Ways my purple secret, and he spread it in the office. That night Colonel Cunningham, who was presently to retire as managing editor, paused on his way through the city-room to compliment me officially.

I sold verse during the following Winter to *Life*, to *Leslie's Weekly*, to the *National Magazine* and to the *New England Magazine*, but in the main I wrote short stories, and most of them landed eventually in magazines. In an old account-book I find a record of my operations: it is interesting chiefly because it shows that the magazines I attempted are nearly all long gone and forgotten, for example, the

---

[2] He wrote vaudeville sketches and dialogues for Dutch, Irish and Jewish comedians, and had a large following. Later on he abandoned that art for the book business, and is at present (1941) the publisher of an excellent monthly for bibliophiles.

Criterion, the *Broadway, Judge, Puck*, the *Black Cat, Munsey's, Success, Ainslee's, Leslie's* (the monthly, not the weekly), *Lippincott's*, the *Youth's Companion, McClure's, Everybody's, Pearson's, Golden Days*, the *Critic*, the *World's Work*, the *Century, Hearst's, Town Topics*, the *Metropolitan*, the *Argosy, Harper's Weekly*. Eheu! it is a roll of the noble dead. The *Bookman* under Peck was the best literary monthly the United States has ever seen; *Munsey's, McClure's* and *Everybody's* had immense circulations; the *Youth's Companion* was read by every American boy; the *Black Cat* was " the story-telling hit of the century "; and a barber-shop without *Puck* and *Judge* would have seemed as nude as one without the *Police Gazette*. But now they are all in the shades, and only a few doddering oldsters recall even their names.

The *Criterion*, then edited by Emory Pottle, husband of Juliet Wilbor Tompkins, was the only solvent survivor of the literary movement of the nineties. I banged away at Pottle for a good while without shaking him, but finally he bought a short story called " The Heathen Rage," born of my trip to Jamaica (Chapter V), and after that I sold him others. For one of them, I find by my records, he paid me $51 and for another $34.35. It was a day of close prices. My steadiest customer in the long run, however, was not Pottle, but Ellery Sedgwick, then editor of *Frank Leslie's Popular Monthly* and later to be editor of the *Atlantic*

Monthly. Sometime in 1901 he bought two of my short stories, and thereafter he bought others. Moreover, he sent me criticisms of those he rejected, and then, as later on, I learned a lot from him. He also put me to work writing articles under the *nom de plume* of John F. Brownell. *Leslie's* was illustrated, and Sedgwick would first pick up a good series of photographs, and then have me write a text to fit them. One such series, as I remember, had to do with the Hagenbeck Zoo at Hamburg. I had never been to Hamburg (and, in fact, never got there until 1938), but I was by now a journeyman reporter, so I did an article that apparently pleased the readers of *Leslie's,* and Sedgwick offered me a job on his home-office staff. The salary he named was more than I was getting on the *Herald,* and he proposed to add a round-trip railroad pass to Baltimore once a month, but I declined at once, for I had already made up my mind that I didn't want to live in New York. Many other offers to move there came later, and beginning with 1914 I actually had an office in the town for twenty years on end, but I stuck to living in Baltimore, which suited me, and still suits me, precisely. While I was an editor of the *Smart Set* and then of the *American Mercury* I commuted to New York as often as weekly, but I stayed at the Algonquin, and never had any permanent quarters.

I was reasonably successful as a writer of short stories, and sold virtually every one I wrote, though not always at the first attempt. One of my good markets was *Short Stories*, and I also had a welcome from Karl Edwin Harriman, then editor of the *Red Book*. Toward the end of 1901 I sold two stories to the *Youth's Companion* that somehow got pigeon-holed in the office, and were not exhumed and published until more than thirty years later. At that time the editor sent me proofs of them, and invited me to make any changes that a generation of experience might suggest, but I passed them without changing a word. They were on the bad side as stories, but they were no worse than the general. Until I joined the staff of the *Smart Set* as its book reviewer, in 1908, I had sold it but one piece of copy — a poor little triolet — and even that never got into the magazine, for I discovered at once that I had already used it in my *Herald* column, and had to recall it. Between 1899 and 1902 I must have bombarded the *Smart Set* with at least forty other pieces of verse, always in vain.

How I managed to find time for all this writing, considering the heavy work I was doing for the *Herald*, I simply can't tell you. My output during my first years on the staff, in and out of the office, was really enormous, for in addition to my short stories and doggerels, I wrote a great many articles for other papers, and began work on a novel. The novel, happily, never got very far. Its scene was Elizabethan England, and Shakespeare was to have been one of the characters. It blew up when I discovered that I knew no more about Elizabethan England than about the M. M. III age of Crete. I was constantly turning up news and feature stories in Baltimore that were of interest in other cities, and selling them there. The first paper I thus broke into was the Philadelphia *Inquirer*, and it was soon followed by the New York *Morning Telegraph*, and then, after a while, by the New York *Sun*. My contributions to the *Sun* were mainly interviews with an imaginary Civil War colonel from the Eastern Shore of Maryland, who was supposed to be the world's greatest authority on the mint julep. Unless my memory plays me false they started that controversy about the proper compounding of the julep which still rages.

Nor did I confine myself, in my reachings out for fresh fields and lusher pastures, to this great Republic. There was in New York in those days a Rhinelander named Henry W. Fischer who made a living translating news items from the chief European papers, and selling them in the United States. The cable service of the time was much leaner than it is today, so there was room for him. It occurred to me that I might set up a similar service from the Far East, and to that end I approached various newspapers in that region, offering to send them occasional American letters in return for the right to mine their news columns. A number bit, and in a little while I was the American correspondent of the Hongkong *Press*, the Kobe *Chronicle*, the Nagasaki *Press*, and the *Ceylon Observer* of Colombo, and had letter-heads printed to prove it. Unfortunately, I soon learned that very few American newspapers were interested in Far Eastern news, and my cash takings remained scanty. Finally, I decided to go to New York to consult Fischer, with a view to an amalgamation. I found him in carpet-slippers at his home in Bensonhurst, and remember clearly his brief comment when I recited to him the list of my papers. It consisted of the single word " Jesus! " But we quickly came to terms, and the amalgamation was effected on the spot. That is to say, I gave him my business, such as it was, and he returned to Manhattan with me and took me to Lüchow's in Fourteenth street, where he bought me an excellent lunch and half a dozen horns of Würzburger.

I have said that I never met any of the recognized literati of Baltimore, but I should mention one exception. He was Jean Havez, who had been a reporter on the *Evening News* only a short time before, and was now eminent as the author of " Goodbye, Booze! ", " Everybody Works But Father," and " He Cert'n'y Was Good to Me," all of them great popular successes. Havez was of French parentage, and a fellow of huge bulk, powerful thirst, and notable amiability. Whenever he returned to Baltimore from Broadway for a visit to the home folks there was a party that lasted for days. While one of them was going on, toward the end of 1900, Lew Dockstader came to town with his minstrel company, and tried to induce Jean to write some local stanzas for his songs. But Jean was too busy to fool with such chicken feed, and for some reason that I forget turned the job over to me. I wrote the stanzas in a few hours, and went to Ford's Opera House that night to hear Lew sing them, full of agreeable anticipations. But he had got an overdose of Jean's party during the afternoon, and when he came upon the stage it was apparent to the judicious that he was not altogether himself. In consequence, he made a horrible mess of my poor jocosities, but the customers roared none the less, for a theatre audience will always laugh at the mention of a familiar name by a comedian, no matter how idiotic the joke he makes on it. Later in the week Lew pulled himself together and did better, and after the Saturday matinée he handed me $10 for my labor. A month later I collared another ten-spot by doing parodies for a Democratic mass-meeting.

But though all these extra-mural activities brought in money, and I was soon earning more outside the office than in it, I began to be conscious of a lack of direction, and tried a number of times to decide formally what I really wanted to do, and to get on with the doing of it. Such advice as I sought usually turned out to be bad, and in consequence I did a great deal of wobbling. I tried all

sorts of things, including even advertising writing,
but they satisfied me as little as the concoction of
verse, which had begun to pall dismally. My short
stories, as I have said, were doing pretty well, and
I got some comfort and solace in the writing of
them from another youngster in the office, Leo
Crane by name and secretary to the managing
editor by trade. Crane was writing short stories
too, and making *Harper's* with them, which was
even better than I was doing. But it gradually
dawned on me that fiction was not my *forte*, and I
did none after 1902. The Boston lemon-squeezer,
Richard G. Badger, tried to inveigle me, in that
year, into letting him bring out a volume of my
stories, but when, after a considerable correspondence, I discovered that he expected me to pay for it,
I fled from his blandishments. He gave me to understand that he thought me one of the coming
masters of the short story in America, but I was
already in grave doubt about that. For two years
I let the matter lie there. Then, through the
theatre, I became interested in George Bernard
Shaw, and through Shaw I found my vocation at
last. My first real book, begun in 1904, was a volume on his plays and the notions in them, critical
in its approach. It was the first book about him
ever published, and it led me to begin a larger volume on Nietzsche in 1907, and to undertake a book
on Socialism two years later, in the form of a debate with a Socialist named La Monte, now rec-

usant and forgotten. After that I was a critic of ideas, and I have remained one ever since.

In all probability, my various false starts did me no harm, though I was undoubtedly delayed in coming to fruit by trying to do too many things at once. My work for the *Herald* was enough in itself to keep one man busy, and I recall many times when I finished a day so nearly worn out that I could barely keep my eyes open. More than once I produced 5000 words of news copy between noon and midnight — not in a single continuous story, which might have been easy enough, but in a miscellany of perhaps twelve or fifteen, every one of them requiring some legging. The newspaper padrones of that era, like the steel magnates, had not yet discovered that over-long hours greatly diminish the amount of good work done. A little while ago I spent an uncomfortable afternoon going through the files of the *Herald*, reading my contributions to it in 1900 and 1901. I discovered that I had done a great deal of shabby writing, full of clichés and banalities. But it was well regarded in the office at the time, and was at its worst appreciably better than the work of many of my colleagues. Not until a somewhat later date did anything properly describable as good writing become the rule on the *Herald*. At least half the members of the staff had literary ambitions of some sort or another, but not one of them ever got anywhere as a writer in the years following. Several took to executive work and became city editors and managing editors, but more became press-agents, and still more left journalism altogether. That is its continuing tragedy : it opens all sorts of outside opportunities to its slaves, and so loses them. I have known newspaper men who have become bank presidents, judges, United States Senators, Governors, generals in the Army, and even bishops. One of the worst who ever lived, Warren Gamaliel Harding, actually became President of the United States. And in Baltimore, during the thirteen years of horror, the best bootician in service was a former newspaper artist.

V

FRUITS OF

DILIGENCE

THE ASSIDUITIES described in the preceding chapters had rewards both subjective and objective, for I not only enjoyed every minute of every day, but also got a good many friendly grunts from Max Ways, and, though I didn't know it, substantial promotion was just around the corner. Unhappily, my hustling bore rather heavily upon a constitution that had some holes in it, and so early as the Spring of 1900 I began to lose weight, and to show other symptoms of exhaustion. From my childhood I had been badgered by disorders of the upper respiratory tract. Every Autumn, on returning to school, I suffered for several weeks from a bleariness that seems, in retrospect, to have been the beginnings of hay-fever, and during my chemical days I picked up a sore throat that stuck to me more or less steadily for ten years.

In most ways, to be sure, I was a perfectly healthy animal, for I could eat and digest anything colorably organic, I recovered quickly from all minor wounds and infections, and to this day I have never had a headache. But there was always something unpleasant going on in my nose or throat, and it took the faculty a long while, not to mention a considerable shedding of blood, to repair the blunders of Yahweh there, and launch me on the robustness that marked my thirties and forties. How many times I went on the table I don't recall precisely, but it must have been half a dozen at least. My tonsils were removed no less than twice — a complete impossibility, as I well know, but nevertheless I was present both times. Even after all that butchery hay-fever remained, and it was not until I was fifty years old that it ever showed any sign of yielding — whether to the vaccines that I was taking by the pint or to the belated mercies of higher powers I do not know.

When, in June of 1900, the fatigues of a hard Winter began to blossom into downright debility, I waited on our old family physician, Dr. Z. K. Wiley,[1] and he talked so mysteriously and so dolefully about tuberculosis that I got alarmed, and rushed off at once to a specialist downtown. This specialist was a competent journeyman of the tran-

[1] He is dealt with at length in Chapter VII of Happy Days.

sition stage between sweet spirits of nitre and the barbituric acid compounds: he was enough of a modernist to wear the first white coat I had ever seen on a doctor in private practise, but he stuck to a carpet on the floor of his surgery, and there was a huge (and rusty) static electricity machine in a corner. He listened to my chest sounds for half an hour or so, pulled down a couple of books, meditated profoundly, and then said that if I wanted to keep out of trouble I had better take a sea voyage, preferably in a sailing ship. His precise diagnosis, whatever it was, he did not mention, and I never learned it afterward, though I assumed that he had heard something upsetting in my bronchial tubes, or maybe even my lungs. There were craft sailing out of Baltimore, he went on, that offered what I needed in a very cheap and convenient form. They were the small schooners that went to the Bahamas every Spring to bring back pineapples. They were not licensed to carry passengers, but he reckoned that my newspaper connections would enable me to get rid of that difficulty.

When I brought this advice to Max Ways he was full of sympathy, and proceeded immediately to practical aid. I had two weeks vacation coming to me, and to them, he said, he would add another week to make up for the days off that I had lost. (I had actually lost at least fifteen, but let it go). Furthermore, if I wanted to add a fourth week I might take it without salary: beyond that he could not go without risking a row with the business office. This seemed fair to me, and Max added to my gratitude by ordering our shipping reporter to go down to the wharves at once, book passage for me on the next pineapple schooner to sail, and arrange the matter of the passenger license with his friend Bill Stone, the collector of customs. The shipping reporter came back presently with the news that the last schooner of the season had cleared that very morning, but he added consolingly that there was a banana boat sailing for the West Indies in two days, and that Old Man Buckman, the Baltimore banana king of the time, was willing to let me sign on it as supercargo. My duties and wages would be nothing, and if I paid $2.50 a day for my transportation and subsistence it would be enough.

I went down to Bowley's Wharf the next morning to have a look at the banana boat. It was a small British tramp of the kind that used to be rolled out along the Clyde as Fords were later to be littered along the River Rouge. Such paint as it showed was in patches of different colors, all of them hideous, and the only members of the crew in sight were a couple of Chinamen. It was the *Ely* of Cardiff, Captain Corning, and only the other day I went through a dusty old book at the Baltimore Customshouse to learn its official specifications. Its registered tonnage, I found, was 541 tons,[2] and it carried a crew of nineteen men. But as it lay there at Bowley's Wharf on that far-off June morning, gradually disgorging its cargo of green bananas, it loomed high above the express wagons on the quay, and seemed almost oceanic beside the bumboats that clustered about it. The heady smell of the tropics gushed from it, and as I gaped at it a strange-looking yellow-faced man in white duck clothes and a Panama hat came out of Old Man Buckman's office and went aboard. Only a few months before I had read Lafcadio Hearn's " Two Years in the French West Indies," and now the glamor of it rose up to enchant me all over. I had never been to sea, and here I was making ready to sail not only the great Atlantic but also the romantic Caribbean. In ten days or less I'd be loitering beneath the palm trees, and plucking bananas, cocoanuts, pineapples, oranges, lemons, limes, coffee, chocolate, nutmegs, cinnamon and allspice from the vine.

I recall nothing of our departure: my first recollection is of the sneaking, poisonous roll of the Atlantic outside the Chesapeake capes. We cleared the capes during the night, and when I came on

2 I take this from the clearance papers, but should add that Captain Corning told me the tonnage was 800. There are, in fact, four sorts of tonnage — the net, which is lowest; the gross, the deadweight, and the displacement, which is highest. Inasmuch as port charges are commonly based on tonnage, the masters of tramp steamers pretend to the lowest that the customs authorities will tolerate. The tonnage of large passenger liners, of course, is reckoned as liberally as possible, to fetch customers.

deck next morning we were already out of sight
of land. To Captain Corning the day was fair and
the sea calm, but not to me. In brief, I was sea-
sick, and after I had refused breakfast and made a
couple of melancholy trips to the *leeward* rail (I
had read enough maritime literature to know *that*)
the good captain unearthed a dilapidated deck-
chair, had it taken up to the starboard wing of the
bridge, and invited me to use it. The air up there,
he said, was fresher than below, and I'd thus recover the quicker. I lolled in the chair all day and
all the following night, with my mouth open and
my eyes rolling, and was still full of misery the
next morning, but toward midday I began to recover, and by the second night I was on my legs
again, and very hungry. What I needed now, said
the captain, was some physic, so he got out his
medicine-chest and handed me a pill — the largest
and blackest, I believe, ever seen on earth. Its effects were almost those of siege artillery, but it did
me no harm, and I was presently sitting on the
after-deck eating a plate of clam chowder with the
captain.

It was his theory that clam chowder was the
queen of all human victuals, and he ate it in large
bowls every day. He said he bought it in cans,
which was reassuring, for I had taken a look into
the galley, and the Chinese cook, naked to the waist
and barefooted, was certainly not appetizing.
While we thus ate our first meal together (there

was nothing beyond the chowder save crackers and bananas) a strange shape suddenly appeared from the depths of the ship. It was that of a skinny old man wearing greasy dungarees and carpet slippers, and showing four or five days' growth of gray beard. His right arm was extended and from his hand hung a strip of what appeared to be bacon — held as gingerly as one might hold a dead rat by the tail. It turned out that he was the Scotch chief engineer, and that he had a complaint. " Is this the sort of meat," he croaked, " to feed a British crew? " " What's the matter with it? " demanded the captain. " There's worms in it," said the chief engineer. " How do you know? " said the captain. " I bit into one," said the chief engineer. " Well, then," said the captain, " spit it out and go to Hell. Back to your engine-room! "

The captain appeared to be glad of my company, for the commander of a British ship is a lonely man, and we ate together for the remainder of the voyage. It lasted eight days altogether — six days to Port Antonio on the north coast of Jamaica, and two days up the coast and back. The total distance covered was something under 1800 miles, but the *Ely* had been built, not for speed but for economy, and it took a brisk tail wind to lift her to nine knots. On the fourth day we passed the little island of San Salvador, where Columbus first sighted America, and the captain made a course close inshore, so that I could see the cairn on the

beach that marks the most fateful landfall in all
history. We were among the islands after that,
with great masses of yellow seaweed floating by on
the ever bluer water, and flying-fish leaping among
them, and strange birds coming out to have a look.
On a day so bright that it was blinding I caught
glimpses of both Cape Maysi, Cuba, and the western mountains of Haiti, but it was not until the
next morning, just before daylight, that we made
Port Antonio. The east began to show streaks of
pink as we entered the little harbor, and so I got
my first sight of the tropics in the vast splendors
of dawn.

It was a spectacle so superb that I stood on deck
silent and almost abashed. As the sun cleared the
horizon and its first rays broke through the palms
of Upper Titchfield they picked up a thousand
gaudy hues, and in a few minutes the whole scene
was shimmering like the image in a kaleidoscope. I
had always thought of the tropics as luxuriant, but
somehow, despite the word-painting of Hearn, I
had overlooked their magnificent color. Now I got
all that color with the light exactly right, and behind it, gradually fading into blue and gray,
stretched the immense escarpment of the Blue
Mountains, just short of a mile and a half high.
And down from the heights, borne by the land-
breeze of the dawn, came the indescribable trop-
ical smell — half sweet and half sour, laden with
strange and lovely scents, but also with whiffs of

decay. I was brought back to the rusty and decrepit *Ely* by the clatter of oar-locks: a small boat was making out from the shadows of the shore. When it came close I saw a very impressive man standing in its stern — coal black as to complexion, but clad in immaculate white ducks and a sun helmet. He was some sort of port functionary, and he entered upon an official parley with the captain. " How many? " I heard him bellow, and the captain bawled back " Nineteen officers and hands and one passenger." Passenger? Wasn't I on the ship's papers as supercargo? The captain recalled the fact instantly and corrected his report. " I meant to say," he howled, " *twenty* officers and hands, and *no* passengers." The functionary made no reply, and I was soon preparing to go ashore.

But at the last minute the captain proposed that I stay aboard while he ran up the coast to load bananas, and in an hour we were off. How far we went I have forgotten, but I recall going ashore at a little place called Port Maria, and wandering through a village that looked precisely like an African kraal, even to the high-pitched thatched roofs and the stilts under the wicker houses. The captain went along and we palavered with the females of the settlement, and watched their naked children at play, while the bucks hauled bananas out to the *Ely* in surf-boats. When it was time for us to return to the ship there was a warning blast of its siren, and all the children dived under the houses. We got back to Port Antonio on the second morning following, again at dawn, and I saw the show of light and color all over again. The *Ely* did not enter the harbor, but only slowed down outside, and I went ashore in a surf-boat, along with four or five banana-checkers of the white race, and a dozen black roustabouts. One of the checkers was a ventriloquist, and he entertained the rest of us by evoking sepulchral shrieks of "Help!" and "Murder!" from the depths of the Caribbean, and turning the livers of the poor Afro-Jamaicans to water.

When we parted the captain and I agreed to meet again in Baltimore on my return, and we did so a couple of months later. I took him to lunch and he asked for clam chowder: he was still eating it every day. He was a Blue Nose from Nova Scotia, and not very communicative, but on this occasion he confided to me an aspiration that, so I learned afterward, was shared by all the merchant masters in the West Indies trade. It was to get a towing line, some happy day, aboard a disabled steamship of large tonnage, and so strike a blow for humanity and collar the captain's share in a juicy pot of salvage. Whether or not this chance for Service ever came to him I never heard, but years afterward, crossing the Atlantic in a luxurious *Doppelschraubenschnellpostdampfer*, I met another captain of the Spanish Main to whom it had. He was a Dane from Schleswig, and his share of the honorarium, so he told me, ran to $30,000. He invested it in certain mysterious speculations in the Oriente province of Cuba, and when I encountered him he had on a Panama hat that had cost him $125 wholesale, and was passing out Upmann cigars at least eight inches long.

I put in a couple of weeks roving and seeing Jamaica, and was delighted enormously by its varied but always gorgeous scenery. I crossed the island on a train that ducked through twenty-four tunnels in forty miles, and between them ran along gorges thick with bamboo and brilliant with crocuses of a hundred colors and a thousand patterns. On another train I traveled westward over the high country, and spent a night at the very English hill-station of Mandeville, where I dined on a cut from a pale, bluish joint of island beef, with two vegetables that tasted like stewed hay. I put up at the old Myrtle Bank Hotel in Kingston (soon to be destroyed in the great earthquake of 1907), and there became acquainted with planters' punch, a drink that I have esteemed highly ever since, and also with an exiled native king from the Mosquito Coast, who lived in gloomy splendor on an official solatium of £1 a day and spent all his time trying to grasp the game of billiards. And I went up to Spanish Town, the old capital of the island, and there searched the records for vestiges of my father's mother's people, the McClellans, who had lived in Jamaica nearly a century before.

These records were in charge of a colored intellectual who wore the thick spectacles with Oxford frames that still mark a learned blackamoor in the British West Indies. He brought out a dozen elephant folios from his catacombs, and deputed a lowly clark, a mulatto with sandy hair, to help me explore them. All the clark and I could find was the will of my great-great-uncle, Jeremiah, who had died in Kingston back in the early forties. He had left, it appeared, a small legacy to my grandmother, then still a child, but whether she ever got it I do not know : I suppose that I must assume that she did, for his executor was a clergyman. This Jeremiah never married, but there was in him none the less a strong strain of philoprogenitiveness, and I discovered that his descendants were numerous all over the southern parishes of the island, and that some of the latest generation had reverted to an almost burnt cork complexion. On my return to Baltimore I spread the news, and acquired thereby a standing in the inner Confederate circles of the town that was very useful to me in my later newspaper work.

Kingston itself was an ancient and romantic town, and I spent some agreeable mornings wandering along its sea-front or rambling through its market, which swarmed with native farmers from back in the brush. They offered all sorts of comestibles that were new to me — for example, cacao beans, plantains, mangoes, and cashew nuts, all of them still unknown in the United States. They had heaps of pimento berries, from which allspice is made, spread out on newspapers, and here and there was a country butcher with rounds and chops of goat meat. I learned to smoke and like the dark, spicy Jamaican cigars, and I had a colored tailor sitting at his booth by the market place make me a suit of white ducks. They were ready in two hours and cost £1, then the standard price for a Class A suit in Kingston. The tailor told me that he had other and cheaper models, some as low as eight shillings, but that he never recommended them to distinguished visitors. I also made acquaintance with a Jamaican soft-drink called cola — the progenitor, I suspect, of Coca-Cola, which was yet concealed in the womb of time. And, as a fanatical Kiplingite, I was enchanted to observe Mulvaney, Learoyd and Ortheris, direct from " Soldiers Three," strutting along the streets of the town with their swagger sticks, tomcatting the more likely black gals, and taking their ease in the less refined bars.

All these studies and recreations were very pleasant, but my time was running short, so I shoved back to Port Antonio to find a ship for home. I learned at once that a Norwegian tramp of about the size and speed of the *Ely* would be clearing in a few days, and I booked passage at once. The next day was a Sunday, and I resolved to spend it sitting on the veranda of the old Titchfield Hotel, listening to the gabble of the super-cargoes, plantation overseers and English remittance men who then constituted the society of the place. They started off after breakfast with a series of magnificent tales of love, trading and carnage, for it was not often that they encountered a new listener who was really eager to listen. But suddenly, in the midst of a hair-raising anecdote about cannibalism in Haiti, two of them rose quietly and faded away, and then two more followed, and then three, and in half a minute I was alone with the raconteur, an Irishman who claimed to be the son of a Spanish duke. Finally, even *he* made off at a quick sneak, and I looked behind me anxiously, almost expecting to see a crocodile bearing down, or even a shark. But all I could find was an old man with a long white beard, buttoned up in a black frock coat of the vintage of 1880. He looked harmless enough, certainly, but I was soon to learn that he was the most dangerous carnivore on the island, for what he packed was a messianic delusion.

In brief, he was tortured by a libido to save the souls of carnal wayfarers, and in order to feed and furnish it he maintained at his own expense a Methodist chapel down in the town. The cost was no burden to him, for he had come to Jamaica back in the first days of the banana business, and picked up plenty of easy money. Now his whole time was given over to his missionarying, and every Sunday

morning he swooped down on the Titchfield veranda and tried to round up the damned assembled
there. As I learned afterward, only strangers
somewhat gone in liquor ever succumbed to him,
and when they got back from his services they always reported a terrible experience. Being sober
at the time, I resisted, and inasmuch as I was already something of an amateur theologian, and
hence familiar with all the classical grips and grap-
ples, I resisted to some effect. But I am glad to testify today, after so many years, that never in this
life have I gone to the mat with a tougher evangelist. He beat any Christian Scientist ever heard
of, or any Presbyterian, however ferocious, or any
foot-wash Baptist. I have been tackled in my day
by virtuosi ranging from mitred abbots to the
kitchen police of the Salvation Army, but never
have I had to fight harder to preserve my doctrinal
chastity. Over and over again the old boy got to
my chin or midriff with scriptural texts that had
the impact of a mule's hoof, and when he turned
from upbraiding to cajolery, and began to argue
that my sufferings in Hell would be upon his head, I
almost threw up the sponge. Indeed, if it had not
been for the audience lying in wait (I could hear it
panting behind the jalousies), I'd have gone down
to his gospel mill with him, if only to get rid of him,
but as it was I was in honor bound to resist, and in
the end he gave up in despair, and shuffled off down
the path to the town. The loafers, when they

sneaked back, stood me a communal drink, and I surely needed it. Some years later, on returning to Port Antonio, I was told that the old man had got himself into a wilder and wilder lather as his years advanced, and that he finally prayed himself to death.

The Norwegian tramp that brought me home, though it was as slow as the *Ely* and little if any larger, turned out to be a great deal cleaner and more shipshape. The young captain, who told me that he owned a 3/70ths interest in it, his father an 18/70ths, and his rich Uncle Olaf a 32/70ths, had his wife with him — a handsome and charming blonde from Bergen, with enlightened ideas about eating and drinking, and a flair for interior decoration in the provincial Scandinavian mode. Every chair in the cabin had a knitted tidy on it, and there were window-boxes at all the portholes, with geraniums growing in them. We dined at 1 p.m., which is to say, we *began* to dine at 1 p.m. The meal itself, prepared by an excellent Danish cook, lasted until 3, and then the steward came in with a large Gjedser cheese, a plate of crackers, a pot of coffee and a bottle of Madeira, and we lingered over them until 4 or even 5. The captain and his wife were eager propagandists for the Norwegian *Kultur*, and they told me so much about Ibsen, then still a dubious character in America, that I became, a few years later, Baltimore's recognized authority on the subject, and even went to the length of reading all the plays, including "The Warriors at Helgeland," perhaps the worst play ever written. I blush to say that I can't remember the name of this amiable and excellent pair, though I seem to recall that it was something on the order of Olsen, Jensen, Hansen, Knutson, Halvorsen or Magnussen. They were intelligent and kindly people, and the captain was a brisk and competent mariner.

But even the briskest mariner collides now and then with what the marine insurance policies call an act of God, and this happened to my friend somewhere or other off the Middle Atlantic coast. It was a misty morning, and in consequence he could not leave the bridge, so I climbed up to keep him company. Suddenly there was a thinning of the mist, and a light-ship loomed up off the *starboard* bow. In other words, we were *inside* the light-ship — and maybe only a few yards from the beach. The captain had yanked the wheel out of the quartermaster's hands in a split second, and the ship heeled over alarmingly as we made a quarter turn on the nautical equivalent of a ten-cent piece. We continued due East for two hours at least, and the next morning, though the sky was as clear as crystal, the captain approached the Delaware capes as cautiously as a sheep approaching a coyote, and, in fact, did not venture to enter at all until another ship came along and showed the way.

That my trip to Jamaica had done me any good

did not appear immediately. I was still under-weight, and as Summer faded into Autumn I developed a cough. The specialist, however, professed to believe that his prescription had worked, and I was presently so busy that I forgot my malaises. I wrote three pieces for the *Sunday Herald* on my adventures, illustrated by halftones from photographs that I had bought on the island. I was ready and willing to write three more, or a dozen more, but Colonel Cunningham got rid of me by saying that a stringent economy order had just come up from the business office, and that he'd catch hell if he authorized any more halftones. I continued skinny until 1904, as the frontispiece to this work shows, but after that I gradually picked up weight, and by the time I was thirty I was so rotund that another specialist put me on one of the first of the reducing diets.

VI

THE GOSPEL OF

SERVICE

It was in the month of May, 1901, that I got my
first really juicy out-of-town assignment — and
began to develop in a large way my theory that
Service is mainly only blah. The scene was the
town of Jacksonville, Fla., and I had been sent
there to cover the great fire of May 3, the largest
blaze in American history between the burning of
Chicago in 1871 and the burning of Baltimore in
1904. It destroyed, as I learn from an encyclopedia, no less than 2361 buildings, stretching over
196 city blocks and 450 acres: all I can add to these
statistics is that when I arrived by train, all set to
load the wires with graphic prose, there seemed to
be nothing left save a fringe of houses around the
municipal periphery, like the hair on a friar's head.

Only one hotel was left standing, and, so far as I could discover, not a single other public convenience of any sort, whether church, hospital, theatre, livery-stable, jail, bank, saloon, barber-shop, pants-pressing parlor, or sporting-house.

But what so powerfully reinforced my growing suspicion of Service was not this scene of desolation, but the imbecility of the public effort to aid its ostensible victims. In every American community of Christian pretensions, North, East, South and West, busy-bodies began to collect money and goods for their succor the moment the first bulletins came in, and by the time I reached what was left of the Jacksonville railroad station the first relief shipments were on their way. The *Herald* started a communal subscription at the drop of the hat, and had cabbaged half a carload of eleemosynary supplies before I left for the South. The city editor (not Max Ways, but one of his successors) favored me from hour to hour with dispatches recording the progress of this philanthropy. The first one, I recall, announced that the boys at the Pimlico race-track had contributed 100 second-hand horse-blankets, and on its heels came one reporting that the saloonkeepers of Baltimore had matched them with 100 cases of Maryland rye.

When I took these dispatches to the Mayor of Jacksonville I expected (at least officially) that he would burst into tears and bid me thank the good people of Baltimore for their generosity, but what he actually did was to laugh. I must confess that, at thought of the horse-blankets, I had to smile myself, for the temperature in Jacksonville was rising 80 degrees, and most of the dispossessed householders, white and black, were camping out gaily in their erstwhile backyards, and refreshing themselves with swims in the St. Johns river. The Mayor was amused, but not surprised, for he had telegrams on his desk showing that many other Northern cities were even more idiotic than Baltimore. St. Paul, it appeared, was sending a couple of bales of old fur coats, and Boston was loading a car with oil-stoves. Even some of the nearby towns, though they should have known better, had contributed supplies almost as insane. Thus, a large box of woolen mittens had already come in from Montgomery, Ala., and Winston-Salem, N. C., had sent a supply of the heavy, sanitary red underwear for which it was then famous.

But it was the Maryland whiskey, not the Pimlico horse-blankets, that really flabbergasted the Mayor. He was far from a Prohibitionist, but the fire had given him plenty of worries, and he did not welcome the new one provided by those hundred cases of rye. What would he do with them when they arrived — supposing they escaped the hobos and railroad men on the way? If he distributed them as medical supplies every white man in Jacksonville would be in a state of liquor within an hour, and probably half of the blackamoors. If he put

his town cops to guarding them he would lose his
police force, which was sorely needed. And if he
asked for a detail from the Florida militia, which
was flocking into town from the swamps to the
southward, there would be a military drunk of a
virulence unparalleled since Sherman's march to
the sea, with a good deal of promiscuous shooting.

I had no suggestion to offer His Honor, and left
him. I wrote a column and a half on the scene of
desolation, and then went to inquire of the railroad
men when the first car from Baltimore could be expected. They knew nothing about it, and had
never even heard of it. Indeed, it was not until
hours later that I got a bulletin from Baltimore
saying that it had just started, and in the same bulletin came news that it was now two cars instead of
one. The second, it appeared, was loaded mainly
with medical and chirurgical *matériel*, including a
bale of splints, five gallons of sulphuric ether, half
a ton of bandages, a crate of wooden legs, and
twenty Potter's Field coffins in shooks. Inasmuch
as no one had suffered anything worse than a few
singes in the fire, and all the other survivors were in
robust health and excellent spirits, this shipment
seemed somehow irrational, but figuring out what
to do with it was the Mayor's grief, not mine, and I
confined myself to trying to learn when it would
arrive.

The Mayor, when I saw him again that evening,
was not as put out about the medical supplies as I

expected, for he said that the militiamen from the Everglades would undoubtedly begin shooting one another anon, and it would be handy to have the splints and coffins, if not the wooden legs. But when I told him (as I had just been advised by a latter bulletin) that the freight of the medical car included a dozen cases of champagne, he immediately took a graver view of the situation, and, in fact, showed a considerable perturbation. This seemed unreasonable to me, for I believed the cops and militiamen, all of them unschooled in the ways of the northern Babylons, would probably take to their heels in alarm the moment the first champagne cork popped, but when I said so to the Mayor he replied that a moral question was involved — in brief, that champagne was still regarded by the decent people of Florida as a lecherous drink, and that having it on his hands might embarrass him politically almost as much as having a trunk full of tights. I could see this point of view and even sympathize with it, though I was young at the time, so I proposed to His Honor that he commandeer the champagne the instant it arrived, wrap it in the horse-blankets from Pimlico, and lock it up in the catacombs under City Hall, for such future reference as human ingenuity and the course of events might suggest. Whether or not this was actually done I do not know to the present day, as the narrative following will show.

It was now late at night, and I began to think

about a place to sleep. As I have said, there was only one hotel left standing, and when I got to it I found that it was swamped by guests — some of them newspaper reporters like myself, but most of them insurance adjusters, brick and lumber salesmen, and agents for sprinkling systems and fire extinguishers. They were sleeping five and six in a room, and all the upstairs corridors were full of cots. Every one of the arm-chairs in the lobby had been grabbed by a sleeper, and others were snoring on the dining-room tables. The night-clerk, a very affable fellow, received my importunities politely, but shook his head. Finally, he had a bright idea. Between the lobby and the dining-room there was a small ladies' parlor, and in it was a grand piano, with a heavily embroidered spread covering it. Why not remove the spread, roll it up for a pillow, and then turn in *under* the piano? I'd thus have the whole space beneath the instrument to myself, a larger area than anyone else had, and I'd be protected from the hooves of guests stumbling through the parlor in the dark. The idea seemed magnificent, and in five minutes I was berthed behind the pedals and sound asleep.

Unhappily, I was not booked for an easy night, for before I got halfway through my first dream a squad of moron soldiery took up post on the veranda outside the parlor window, to guard a burned bank across the street, and their simian gabble and guffawing made me toss and moan, dead tired though I was. But the worst was reserved for 3 a.m. or thereabouts. The goofs had brought a primeval machine-gun with them, and one of them, thinking he saw ghouls in the ruins of the bank, suddenly turned it on. With the sounding-board of the piano directly over my head I got the full force of the reverberation — indeed, I got a great magnification of it. It took on the proportions of the explosion of a battleship, and when I fetched up with a start my head banged the hull of the piano, and I got a bump that stuck to me until I was back in Baltimore. The night-clerk patched me up with vinegar and butcher-paper from the kitchen, but I slept no more that night.

All the next day I devoted to badgering the railroad men about the two relief-cars, and all of the day following, with occasional pauses to file instalments of my thriller on the ruins. No report of them had come in. No one had any notion where they were. Meanwhile, my city editor bombarded me with demands that I get and send a statement from the Mayor, setting forth Jacksonville's gratitude. Rather curiously for so philosophical a man, he raised scruples about giving it to me. What if the cars never arrived at all? What if they were wrecked along the way, and the whole world learned that they had not got in? Inspired and goaded by my city editor, I labored with His Honor, and in the end he compromised with his conscience by requiring me to swear that if he gave me a statement

I would not send it until the cars were safe in port.
I was ready, by that time, to agree to anything,
and after a conference with his advisers he produced the document. It turned out, after all that
backing and filling, to be only a carbon of one that
had been dispatched to Savannah, Atlanta, New
Orleans, and various other nearby cities, with the
name of Baltmore inserted in a blank left for the
purpose. It began by saying that the people of
Jacksonville were completely overcome by the astounding generosity and loving-kindness of the
(Baltimore) humanitarians, and would never forget it so long as the pleasant and mutually profitable business relations between Jacksonville and
(Baltimore) continued. It went on in this vein for
500 or 600 words, and then closed with some sly remarks about the salubriousness of the Florida cli-
mate, and the incomparable flavor of the citrus
fruits. This was before the great Florida land
boom, so there was no mention of real estate opportunities, but the general tenor of it was certainly
very complacent, and I heard when I got home that
some of the horse-lovers of Pimlico, on reading it,
said they wished they had kept their blankets.

Armed with the carbon, I spent the evening in
the railroad yards searching for the two cars of
relief supplies, and not finding them. Along about
ten o'clock the fireman of a switching engine told
me that he had seen a couple of suspicious-looking
cars on a siding about a mile out of town, and I

hoofed there to have a look. I got to the place all right, and even found the cars, only to learn that they were two old wrecks loaded with razor-back hog hides from Waycross, Ga. I turned sadly away, and started down the long, long trail back to stricken but contented Jacksonville. I had gone hardly a third of the distance when a yahoo militia-man jumped from behind a gondola, and jammed his bayonet into my front. He was taking his stance to shove it through me when I managed to yell. This set him to yelling too, and in a moment two more privates, a corporal, a sergeant, and finally a lieutenant rushed up. It appeared that the yahoo charged me with looting, though there was nothing within half a mile that any sensible man would loot. I demanded trial on the spot, and it was presently in progress, with the lieutenant serving as both president and judge-advocate. He was an ill-favored fellow, and if he lived to 1934 he probably got a part in " Tobacco Road," but he knew something about the rules of evidence, and so acquitted me with honor, and even offered me a chew from his plug as a solatium.

There ensued three days and three nights of fevered hunting for those cars, gladdened on the afternoon of the third day by a telegram from the Seaboard's division superintendent at Savannah saying that they had been found on a siding near a water-tank called Jones. I tried to wire to Jones, but was told that there was no operator there, nor indeed anything save the tank itself and an old man who spent his time plugging its leaks with rosin. I laid off the third night, and had a fair sleep, and then spent the next morning writing a long piece describing the grateful gloats and sobs of the starving and shivering Jacksonville populace as the cars rolled in, and the supplies were distributed. I figured on filing this palpitating stuff the instant they really arrived, or were reported anywhere below the Georgia frontier, but when they failed to turn up at 6 p.m. I filed it anyhow, and was encouraged two hours later by a complimentary telegram from the home office.

Bucked up by this appreciation, I decided to put in another night in the yards, looking for the cars. When I got there no one had seen them, or heard anything about them, but while I stood talking with the yardmaster, wondering whether I had better give up, they suddenly appeared from nowhere, directly before our eyes. They were running next to the caboose of a way-freight, and how they got there I never learned. The door of one hung by a single hinge, but when it came to a halt I could find no sign that it had been burgled, and the railroad men showed no predatory interest in its contents. On both sides of each car were muslin banners (or what was left of them) reading:

BALTIMORE MORNING HERALD
RELIEF TRAIN FOR
JACKSONVILLE FIRE SUFFERERS

The railroad men snickered quietly at the words " train " and " sufferers," and began pulling the signs down — as I gathered from their talk, to make shirts for their children. I filed the Mayor's long-delayed statement before turning in, and slept late the next morning, for my mission of mercy was over. At noon or thereabout I dropped into His Honor's office, and he promised to do something about the cars as soon as he could come round to it — that is, if the anthropoid militiamen did not seize them meanwhile, and spirit them away to the Everglades. He even suggested politely that if I would stick about a day or two longer a couple of the bottles of Maryland rye would be mine for the asking. But I needed sleep more than stimulants, and, what is more, I was lathering for a square meal, for the catering arrangements at Jacksonville, even disregarding the fire, were much less elaborate in those days than they are today, and I was tired of tough hog-meat and greasy corn-pone. That night I boarded a train for Baltimore, and the next day, at a meal-stop called Norlina, near the border between North Carolina and Virginia, I tackled a platter of country victuals that still sticks in my mind after forty years. It was, in quality, superb, for it consisted principally of chicken fried to perfection, with hominy cakes and cream gravy. In quantity, it was colossal, and the half hour allowed for devouring it was enough to dispose of only about a third of it. The rest, according to the custom of travelers in that age, I stuffed into my pockets, and I was still at work on it when we crossed the James river.

A year later I was sent back to Jacksonville to find out how the town was making out. I found, as I expected, that the fire had been the luckiest act of God in all its history. The marsh that used to lie between it and the channel of the St. Johns river, generating mosquitoes and malaria, was now filled with the debris, and dozens of new warehouses were going up. A little while later Congress ordered the 19-foot channel dredged to 24 feet, and then to 30. During the next decade the population of Jacksonville more than doubled, and today it is a metropolis comparable to Nineveh or Gomorrah in their prime, with the hottest night-clubs between Norfolk and Miami, and so many indigenous salvage-crews of humanitarians that Florida can't contain them, and they are constantly reaching out for more distant clients. When, in 1904, Baltimore itself had a big fire, they proposed to send up enough oranges (some of them almost fresh) to supply 500,000 people for 100 days, but the Baltimore authorities declined them.

My exertions on my mission seem to have been well received in the *Herald* office, for during the following year I was given a number of other interesting out-of-town assignments. I recall, for example, being sent to the battlefield of Antietam, in Western Maryland, to cover the dedication of a soldiers' monument by the immortal McKinley. He was to become an angel only a couple of months later, but he did not know it at the time, and so made a roaring speech from an open-air stand on a very hot day. There were scores of reporters present, including a large squad of Washington correspondents wearing cutaway coats and carrying doggy walking-sticks. This was the first time that I had ever come into contact with such eminent journalists, and you may be sure that I gaped at them with every show of respect. Inasmuch as McKinley's secretary, George B. Cortelyou, had brought along copies of the presidential speech, it was not necessary to risk sunstroke by listening to it, so I spent the hour of its delivery roving about the grounds. A large marquee had been erected for the accommodation of distinguished guests, and in it I found a dozen or more United States Senators loading up on fried chicken and champagne. Late in the afternoon the whole party returned to Washington on a special train provided by the Baltimore & Ohio Railroad, and I heard the same Senators go through a long programme of American folk-song, including " The Old Black Bull." There were no ladies present, for in those days the female politician had not yet begun to spoil junkets.

Various assignments took me to Washington, and there came eventually the glorious day when I sat in the Senate press-gallery for the first time.

Like all the really massive experiences of life, it turned out to be more or less disappointing. I also made a number of trips to Annapolis, to help my betters cover the Maryland Legislature, and there I sniffed for the first time the peculiar smell that radiates from all such bodies — that sickening mixture of stale beer and free lunch, contributed by the city members, and cow and sweat, contributed by the yokels. In the years since I have smelled it in six or eight other state capitals, and have never been able to detect a difference of more than two per cent. between one and the next. But the best of all the assignments that came to me in those happy days, and indeed the best of my whole career on newspapers, I had to miss. It was the Martinique volcano story of 1902. The first blow-off of Mont Pelée, of course, happened too suddenly to be covered, but when the Navy started a couple of rescue ships for the island there was room on them for a few reporters, and Carter got a place for the *Herald*, and assigned me to it. The boys on those rescue ships saw the most stupendous spectacle ever staged on earth, for when they heaved in sight of the island the volcano went off again, and with ten times the violence of the first time. The ships were rocked by the blast and covered with ashes, but no one was hurt. All the reporters vomited purple copy, and for a week afterward it filled the American newspapers. Alas, none of it was mine, for on the day before the ships sailed I was served with a summons in a lawsuit relating to my father's estate, and my lawyer warned me that if I disregarded it I might land in jail on my return, and my mother might lose a piece of property. No one else was sent.

VII

SCENT OF THE

THEATRE

THE REPORTER covering the theatres for the
Herald, during my first year on the staff, was Theodore M. Leary, a charming young Irishman who
was a graduate of the Johns Hopkins and whose
father, a general in the Army, was commandant at
Fort McHenry, the Baltimore military post. The
job, in those days, was not a full-time one, and
Leary was often given other assignments. In June,
1900, he was sent to Philadelphia to help Al Goodman, the political reporter of the paper, cover the
Republican National Convention. The importance of the job impressed him vastly, and when his
train reached Wilmington he put off a telegram
to Max Ways, announcing the fact. Half an hour

later, having got to Philadelphia, he sent another, reading:

Have arrived safely. Delegates pouring in. Prepare for at least a column and a half tonight.

The waggish Max passed these telegrams around the office, and when Leary returned he was given a heavy dose of kidding. But he threw it off by doing excellent work, and was soon ranked among the four or five best reporters on the paper. Such a youngster, when assigned to the theatres, was always marked, in those days, by the theatrical managers of New York, and in a little while he began to receive offers from this one or that one to go on the road as press-agent of a traveling company. At the beginning of the season of 1901–2 he finally succumbed, and at his suggestion I was given his place. Thus I escaped the City Hall at last, and in the intervals of covering the theatres took general assignments. In October I was made Sunday editor, but continued to do the theatres and also to write for the editorial page.

Baltimore then had two first-class playhouses, Ford's Opera House and the Academy of Music, a third that played dollar shows, a fourth that offered vaudeville, a fifth that had a stock company, a sixth that played only melodrama, and a couple of burlesque houses. There was a change of bill in each of them every week, and every change of bill had to be noticed. The theatre reporter (or, as he was called, the dramatic editor) commonly did the principal attraction of the week, but when Robert I. Carter became managing editor of the *Herald* at the end of 1900 he took over the leading notice himself, for he had formerly been a dramatic critic, was still greatly interested in the theatre, and knew more about plays than any other man I had encountered up to that time. Thus, when I succeeded Leary, it was only the second choice that fell to me, but I was very well content, for two times out of three Carter would pick the more serious plays, which left me the comedies and musical pieces. I recall, for example, that I did " Florodora " when it first came to Baltimore, and liked it so well that I dropped in at every subsequent performance of the week, usually just as the famous sextette was coming on. In the first theatre page that I got out as Sunday editor, the piano score of the sextette was reproduced as a background for a photograph of the six elegant bucks and six gorgeous wenches who danced and sang it.

On Monday evenings, after Carter had dictated his own notice and I had written mine, he would invite me to his office, and instruct me in the technic of reviewing. He believed, and taught me, that a dull notice, however profound, was not worth printing. " The first job of a reviewer," he would say, " is to write a good story — to produce something that people will enjoy reading. If he has nothing to say he simply can't do it. If he has, then it doesn't make much difference whether what he says is fundamentally sound or not. Exact and scientific criticism is not worth trying for, especially on a provincial paper. Don't hesitate to use the actors roughly: they are mainly idiots. And don't take a dramatist's pretensions too seriously: he is usually only a showman." Carter warned me against associating with theatrical people, but added that he meant performers, not authors or managers. In search of material for my daily column of theatrical gossip I tackled all members of the latter two classes who visited Baltimore, and thereby got to know many notables of the time, for example, Daniel Frohman, Victor Herbert, Clyde Fitch, Paul Armstrong, Augustus Thomas, Charles Klein and A. M. Palmer. Charles Frohman I never met. When he came to town he secreted himself mysteriously, and getting to see him was an elaborate business, almost as difficult as seeing the Pope. When, in the end, I was solemnly invited to the felicity of waiting on him, I refused, for I had seen a good many of his plays by that time, and come to the conclusion that he was a fraud.

But I naturally met all of the salient press-agents of the era, for they came to my office as soon as they got to town. Most of them were former newspaper reporters, and all that I can remember were very pleasant fellows. One of the liveliest was a Dane with the strange name of A. Toxen Worm, who stood at the head of the craft but is now forgotten. Another who was good company was a tall, slim, handsome blond young man named Herbert Bayard Swope, who interrupted a successful newspaper career to whoop up the English actor, Martin Harvey. Harvey seemed to me to be a ham, but Swope I came to terms with quickly, and we have been on a footing of mutual esteem and suspicion ever since. In 1912 he was married in Baltimore, and I was best man at his wedding. In 1906 I was drafted for the same delicate office by Channing Pollock, who then combined press-agenting and play-writing, but I had to function *in absentia*, for at the last moment he and Anna Marble decided to be married in Canada. Many other press-agents of that era were interesting and able men, among them, Paul Wilstach, who whooped up Richard Mansfield and actually believed that he was the greatest actor on earth; James Forbes, who labored for many bad stars, including Robert Edeson; Eugene Walter, who did the same, again including Edeson; Bayard Veiller, who represented, among other first-chop performers, his own excellent wife, Margaret Wycherly; and Frank J. Wilstach, who was Paul's elder brother, and served, at different times, De Wolf Hopper, E. H. Sothern, Julia Marlowe, Viola Allen, William Faversham and Mrs. Leslie Carter. These were all clever fellows, and every one of them made his mark in the years following. Paul Wilstach wrote a number of successful plays, accumulated a competence, and retired in bachelor splendor to a romantic old estate on the Potomac. Forbes, in 1906, wrote "The Chorus Lady," which broke records on Broadway; Walter, in 1908, alarmed and delighted it with "The Easiest Way"; and Veiller had two big successes in 1918 and 1928 — "Within the Law" and "The Trial of Mary Dugan." Frank Wilstach wrote no plays, but devoted all his leisure to a dictionary of similes that had a cordial reception when it came out at last, and remains the standard work in its field. He collected its contents as he toured the country ahead of his various troupes, and always carried a large ledger for recording them. I supplied him with scores, including many that I invented on the spot, with modest credit to such authors as Aristotle, Confucius and John Calvin. Frank died in 1933 and Forbes five years later, but the rest still flourish.

In 1902, coming to Baltimore ahead of Robert Edeson, Forbes confided to me that he had planted an illustrated article on his star's achievements at field sports, and asked for my help in making the photographs. Edeson, as a matter of fact, knew no more about field sports than a mother superior, but we soon borrowed an outfit of guns, fishing tackle, shooting jackets, hip boots and so on, and went out to Druid Hill Park with a photographer. The time was mid-morning, and the park was deserted. For the fishing pictures a small pond

114

served as stream, and then Edeson changed to the shooting jacket and began to draw beads on imaginary birds. Suddenly a mounted cop came galloping over a hill, and put the whole party under arrest. He had heard, he said, several shots. Didn't we know that it was a serious offense to shoot birds in a public park? We protested that no shot had been fired, and handed over the gun to prove it. We also offered to let the cop search us for cartridges. But he insisted that he had heard at least three shots from the other side of the hill. Why, else, should he have charged us at a gallop? The mystery was never solved. We finally talked the cop out of calling the wagon, but he went away muttering. To this day his imbecile, puzzled face returns to me in my dreams, and wakes me in a sweat. Druid Hill Park, as every Afro-Baltimorean knows, is infested by witches, but who ever heard of a witch using firearms?

Paul Armstrong I met for the first time when he came to Baltimore to put on his first play, " St. Ann." He had been working for Hearst as a sports reporter specializing in pugilism, and had saved enough money to buy scenery and hire a company. All the regular managers of the time had refused the play, and Armstrong was already full of a loathing for them that continued to his death. It turned out to be a dreadful *réchauffé* of Sardou, Pinero and Augustus Thomas, and the opening performance was a nightmare to both audience and dramatist. One of the principal actors showed up drunk and had to be fired, and then another actor, though sober, undertook to beat up Armstrong for an imaginary insult to the leading woman. Armstrong, who was a tough fellow, knocked out this poor fish, so there were two vacancies in the cast, and when a girl who had a small part began to be saucy she was fired too, and there were three. The first act wobbled, the second was worse, the third became downright maniacal, and the fourth was never finished. These proceedings, and especially the bout between Armstrong and the actor, made excellent newspaper fodder, and it was my sworn duty to describe them in the *Herald*. Armstrong, as a newspaper man, understood my position and did not resent my story. Instead, he seemed grateful that I had tamed it down as much as possible, and we straightway became warm friends. A few years later he was the king of Broadway, with three big successes running at once. Having thus fallen into funds, he decided to become a landed proprietor in Maryland, where, as he used to say, there were more shades of green in Spring than anywhere else on earth. He bought an ancient and dilapidated estate below Annapolis, and moved there with his wife and three little girls, and after that I used to see a lot of him, for I spent many weekends with him and he seldom passed through Baltimore without looking me up.

One day in the Spring of 1915 I received a letter

from him, dated Atlantic City, saying that he was laid up there by a heart attack, and asking me to arrange for his treatment at the Johns Hopkins Hospital. I did so at once, and in a few days he was at the hospital under the care of Dr. Lewellys F. Barker, the successor of Osler as its chief physician. Dr. Barker found that his heart was very badly impaired, and warned him that he'd have to avoid excitement if he expected to live. Armstrong promised solemnly to go on a Mark Twain regimen — doing all his writing in bed, and leaving every sort of business to his confidential agent, Dan Piazzi. But he had hardly got back to New York before he became involved in a lawsuit, and before long he was engaged in his usual fights with actors. By the end of the Summer he was dead. He was a curious man, and had some talent. His plays, to be sure, were mainly trash, but nevertheless they were very adroitly constructed, and he made success after success, some of them record-breaking. Despite his truculent ways and fearsome makeup — he wore a Buffalo Bill goatee and a two-gallon hat, and liked striking clothes and flashy jewelry — he was a simple-minded fellow at bottom, and more than once, listening to him expound the plot of a new play at his dinner-table, I have seen tears roll down his cheeks. He probably earned more money than any other dramatist up to his time, whether here or in Europe. His revenues from a single one-acter, played by two companies in vaudeville, ran, to my personal knowledge, beyond $2000 a week for two years on end. He was preparing, in his last days, to invade the movies in the grand manner, and if he had lived ten years more he'd have died a multi-millionaire, for he was already master of all the eye-popping, heart-breaking and liver-scratching devices that the movie Shakespeares were to develop only long afterward. At least five years before D. W. Griffith exacerbated the soul of humanity with " The Birth of a Nation " Armstrong was entertaining me with projects for historical films on twice its scale, with such excursions and alarms in them that they would have paled it. He died at forty-six, leaving three widows. Both of the two that I knew were beautiful and charming women.

I met a great many other dramatic authors in those days, and also most of the current composers of operettas and musical comedies. Reginald De Koven I remember mainly for the fact that he was in liquor every time I had him under my eye, and Victor Herbert because of his marked German accent. Herbert had been brought up in Stuttgart, where his mother had married for the second time, and he looked, talked and carried himself far more like a Württemberger than like the Irishman that he was. He spent a couple of Summers in Baltimore as the director of pop concerts. A man of large bulk, with a neck that required a No. 20 collar, he suffered much from the heat. I used to drop in on him between numbers, and usually found him sitting in his dressing-room in his undershirt, drinking Rhine wine and damning the thermometer. During one especially hot spell he wrecked four or five shirts of an evening, and had to put on a fresh collar after every number. Once, to make conversation, I asked him how he had got the idea for the lovely gipsy love-song in " The Fortune Teller." He replied that he didn't know. " I was aware," he said, " that Eugene Cowles would sing it, and when I sat down to write it I had his voice in mind. After that, I just wrote it." Another popular composer of the time, Willard Spenser, told me that he fetched up melodies by improvising at a church organ. This Spenser was a tall, cadaverous fellow with wispy side-whiskers, and looked more like a Presbyterian deacon than a composer for the theatre. He was, in fact, very prim and pious, and never visited back-stage if he could help it. His two operettas, " The Little Tycoon " and " The Princess Bonnie," were enormous successes, but today they are as teetotally forgotten as " Erminie " or " Fra Diavolo."

It was usual, when a new play had its first performance in Baltimore, for colleagues from New York, Philadelphia and Washington to come to town for the event, and I thus became acquainted with a number of them. One was Acton Davies, of the New York *Evening Sun*, a short, squatty fellow with a high piping voice and a somewhat effeminate manner. One night he appeared for the opening of a new Clyde Fitch play, and after the first act became engaged in a debate in the lobby of Ford's Opera House with the author, whose voice was even higher than his own, and whose manner was even more girlish. Presently they were joined by a Baltimorean who surpassed both of them in both respects. In a few minutes the three were surrounded by an appreciative gallery, and when it began to applaud and wise-crack Charlie Ford had to shut off a possible riot by shooing them into the house. The older dramatic critics, in those days, wore opera cloaks and plug hats, and looked a good deal like melodrama villains. They were mainly ignoramuses, though some of them could write. The dean of the corps was William Winter, of the New York Tribune, who would sometimes take three of the wide columns that his paper then affected to review a Shakespearean performance. Four-fifths of his critique, of course, was written in advance, and consisted of a pedantic discourse on the play. He was a violent opponent of all novelty in the theatre, and spent his last years denouncing Ibsen, Hauptmann and Shaw. He died in 1917, aged eighty-one. If he had lived into the Eugene O'Neill era he'd have suffered so powerfully that his death would have been a kind of capital punishment.

Winter, like most of the other dramatic critics of the time, tried to write plays himself, but never

with any success. There were, however, a few of
the brethren who kept resolutely on their own side
of the footlights. To be precise, there were two
that I knew of — Stuffy Davis of the New York
Globe and myself. In 1903 we organized a national association called the Society of Dramatic
Critics Who Have Never Written Plays, and began to hold quarterly conventions in Brown's
Chophouse, in New York, then the chief boozing-
ken of theatrical business men. We got friendly
notice in the stage weeklies, and several other colleagues applied for membership, but it always
turned out, on investigation, that they had plays
under way in secret, and were thus frauds. Stuffy
kept the oath of the organization until his lamented
death, but soon afterward I succumbed so far as to
write a couple of one-acters. I consoled my conscience, which was still functioning more or less in
those days, by maintaining that they were unplay-
able. When they were actually played I began to
wobble, and in 1919 I had wobbled so far that I
wrote a full-length play in collaboration with
George Jean Nathan. But though Nathan thus
sinned with me, he professed to support the principles of the Davis-Mencken society, and the two
of us cleared our skirts by refusing to let the play
be done on Broadway. One manager offered us
$10,000 cash for the refusal of it, but we had gone
too far by then to turn back, and had to say no.
To this day it has never been played.

One of the most competent young dramatic editors of the early century was Will A. Page, of the Washington *Post*. In the Autumn of 1901, soon after I had taken over the job in Baltimore, he moved there to be press-agent for a new stock company organized by George Fawcett. Fawcett was an educated and intelligent man, and his company soon made a big success. His beautiful wife, Percy Haswell, was the competent leading woman, and the leading man was Frank Gillmore, a handsome young Englishman who was later to become the head of Actors' Equity. The stage manager of the company was Percy Winter, old William's son, and its youngest member was a youth named Frank Craven, afterward to be well known as both actor and dramatist. The Fawcett company opened in " The Liars " and then proceeded to a series of other plays of the same amusing and civilized sort. Almost every night I dropped in at the theatre for a palaver with Page, and he was soon reinforcing Carter's attempt to make me take the drama seriously. It was from him that I first heard of George Bernard Shaw, and he fanned my interest in Ibsen, first set going by the episode described at the end of Chapter V. One day at the beginning of the season of 1902–3 he asked me if I thought that the Baltimore public would stand for a production of Ibsen's " Ghosts," which had been recently suppressed in London and was poison to all the current William Winters. I was naturally hot for it, and

on November 12 the play was put on, with Mary
Shaw as Mrs. Alving, Frederick Lewis as Oswald,
Maurice Wilkinson as Pastor Manders, Charles A.
Gay as Engstrand, and Virginia Kline as Regina.

The first night was somewhat exciting, for the
house manager, misunderstanding the action,
jumped to the conclusion that Mrs. Alving was
trying to seduce Oswald, and rushed out of the
house exclaiming " We'll all go to jail! " The next
day the critic of the *Sun* deplored " the revolting
theme " and " the ghastly story," and the *American* and *News* lamented that such immoral and
pathological stuff should be shown in a Christian
city, but, with Carter's eager approval, I beat the
drum for it in the *Herald*, and Baltimore received
it without any further sign of moral trauma. It
had, in fact, a good week, and after that the cast
presenting it was detached from the Fawcett company and took it on the road. First and last, it was
shown for three years. Other plays of pathological
and subversive flavor were added to the little
troupe's répertoire, but " Ghosts " remained its
stand-by. Miss Shaw not only played it in scores
of remote towns, some of them deep in the Bible
Belt; she also lectured on it at many bucolic colleges, and always escaped without encountering
anything worse than a few bewildered belches.
From time to time fresh actors were thrown into
the male parts, but Virginia Kline stuck to the end.

The " Ghosts " week was the high point of the

Fawcett company. Page tried to get the American rights to the early Shaw plays, and had a brisk correspondence with Shaw on the subject, but they could not come to terms. In 1903 he left the company, and when business turned bad Fawcett resorted to such obvious boob-squeezers as " The Three Musketeers," " Monte Cristo " and " Blue Jeans." When he quit at last he was succeeded by a manager of such small experience in the theatre that he was constantly appealing to newspaper men for advice. I was promoted to city editor at about the same time, and was followed as dramatic editor by a smart young reporter named Eugene Bertram Heath, who quickly became this manager's chief confidant and fatal curse. When Heath first came to work on the *Herald* a careless city editor, remembering only that his given name was somewhat romantic, entered him on the payroll as Percy, and Percy he remained to the end of his days. He lived to do the American book of " Sari," a great musical success, and to become a considerable figure in Hollywood. His counsel to Fawcett's unhappy heir and assign was chiefly waggish. Noting that the leading woman of the company was a blonde of large curves, he suggested that she be cast as Hamlet, *à la* Sarah Bernhardt. The manager fell for it — and to everyone's astonishment the week showed good takings. Percy then proposed satirically that her talents be turned loose upon " The Two Orphans," and when it, too, showed a profit, he advised that it be followed by a different version of the same play. The result was a gay and delirious week, for the actors trying to play the second version could not forget the first, and wallowed in confusion from curtain to curtain. Percy will appear again in Chapter XV. He was a man of parts. Unhappily, he had taken on family responsibilities, and when a good offer to go on the road as a press-agent came to him he accepted it, and Baltimore knew him no more.

I naturally received such offers myself, but I always refused them, for I was determined to stay in Baltimore. One of those offers was from E. H. Sothern. It was harder to resist certain more subtle approaches. Once I got word that David Belasco, then at the height of his celebrity, desired my opinion on a play, and it was hinted that he would expect to pay a substantial honorarium for it. I declined without thanks, for I regarded Belasco as a mountebank, and knew that what he wanted was not my judgment on a play but my support for all his trashy enterprises. The attempts of local managers to fetch me sometimes almost succeeded. When Charlie Ford would call me up at home, and tell me with trembling voice that a traveling press-agent was too drunk to function, and ask me in God's name to take over his work for a couple of days, I was unpleasantly tempted, but my natural cynicism always came to my aid, and I ducked. There were also blandishments from actors, but here it was easier going, for I knew very few of them, and never had anything to do with them. Once, after I had written a somewhat tart notice of Richard Mansfield's performance in Schiller's " Don Carlos," he invited me to dine with him on his private car and favor him with my notions in more detail, but I replied that I was too busy to come. He thereupon sent me a large photograph of himself, elegantly inscribed.

My general view of the theatre, in truth, was always somewhat skeptical. I continued to do an occasional review even after I became city editor, and when the *Herald* blew up at last and I transferred to the *Sun* I became its principal reviewer, though not its dramatic editor. Not many plays of any real interest came out in those days. The favorite dramatists were such cheap jacks as Clyde Fitch and Charles Klein, and the dominant managers were such charlatans as Charles Frohman, Belasco, and Klaw and Erlanger. During the Winter of 1905–6, working for the *Sun*, I wrote twenty-three unfavorable notices in a row. Charlie Ford thereupon complained bitterly that I was ruining his business, and protested that he was not to blame, for he had to take whatever plays the Theatrical Trust sent him. On reflection, I found myself sympathizing with him, and thereupon asked to be relieved. I have never written a line of dramatic criticism since.

VIII

COMMAND

When Carter appointed me Sunday editor toward the end of 1901 I was as green as grass, and made heavy weather of it for the first few weeks. It may seem strange, but I can't recall the name of the man I succeeded. Whoever he was, he must have left the office as well as the job, for I got no instruction from him, and had to find my own way. In those days, as in these, reporters were taught nothing about printing, nor even about make-up, and it was rare for one of them to so much as peep into the composing-room, the engraving department, the stereotype foundry, or the press-room. Thus when I made my appearance in the first-named I was almost helpless. But Joe Bamburger, the foreman, was a sympathetic fellow, and so was his assistant, Josh Lynch, and in a little while they had broken me in. I naturally developed a grateful affection for them, and I think they liked me too, for we remained on friendly terms until both were dead. In a little while we fell into the habit of victualling together every Saturday evening between the time the last page of the Sunday supplement closed and the time the first page of the news section was ready. We always stopped first at a saloon in Fayette street, and there laid in a couple of beers. Then we proceeded to an eating-house in Baltimore street, where the principal dish was a beef stew so nourishing and so cheap that Joe called it the Workingmen's Friend. We ate it every Saturday, to the accompaniment of butter-cakes and coffee, and then returned to the *Herald* office to search the supplement, which was just coming up from the cellar, for bulls. We always found them, and always blamed one another. Joe was a tall, slim, solemn-looking fellow with a black beard, but when the spirit moved him he could swear magnificently. He was a pious Catholic, denounced the new heresy of birth control as mortal sin, and had eleven or twelve children. Josh was short and stout, with a gift for profanity that was more explosive than Joe's, but perhaps fell below it in reach and endurance. Joe would often say: " Josh is an inhuman bluff." Both were first-rate printers, trained in the days before the linotype had reduced printing to the level of typewriting, and I learned more about the newspaper trade from them than I ever learned from anyone in the editorial department with the one exception of Max Ways.[1]

Save on a few metropolitan papers, the Sunday editor of today is not much concerned about his pages of colored comics, for they are supplied by syndicates, and most of them are printed by out-side contractors, far from the office. But in 1901 there were no syndicates, and every paper had to prepare and print its own. This work, untrained as I was, gave me endless torment, for I quickly found that comic artists were a temperamental and nefarious class of men, that engraving depart-ments were never on time, that pressmen had an unearthly talent for printing colors out of regis-ter, so that a blue spot intended to represent an eye usually appeared clear outside the cheek, and that plates plainly marked red were often printed as yellow, and *vice versa.* The first page of the color sheet, in those days, was seldom given over to comics, which were still regarded as somewhat *infra dig.;* its more usual adornment was a large pic-ture of a damsel in an hour-glass corset and trail-ing skirts, labeled " The Summer Girl," " The Spirit of Thanksgiving," or something of the sort. The artists who drew these sugar-teats were even worse characters than the concocters of comics, and needed more policing. If one of them delivered a drawing on schedule he was sure to be *non est* when

1 There is more about them in Chapter XIX following, and yet more on pp. 214 and 215 of my book, Happy Days.

the time came to block out the color plates, and if he did the color plates promptly it always turned out that he had done them wrong. There were weeks when I spent at least two-thirds of my working hours wrestling with these criminals. They were, taking one with another, very affable fellows, and they used to try to mollify me by presenting me with large colored drawings of beautiful gals without any clothes on, but my professional relations with them were usually strained, and it never gave me any pain when I heard that one of them had broken a leg or got soaked for heavy alimony by his wife. Toward the end of 1902, happily for my sanity, syndicated comics began to appear, and I need not say that I subscribed to them with cheers. The very names of the first ones are now forgotten — Simon Simple, Billy Bounce, the Teasers, the Spiegelburgers. Finally came Foxy Grandpa, and we were on our way. Even so, it was necessary to keep a comic artist or two on call, for now and then the business office sold a quarter-page ad on a comic page, and something had to be cooked up to go 'round it. I not only had to supervise the preparation of this home-made stuff, but also to supply the ideas for it. The only ideas that the comic artists of that age ever produced on their own were either too banal to be used, or too lascivious.

Some time ago I put in a gloomy afternoon in the Pratt Library in Baltimore, going through the files of the *Sunday Herald* for the period of my editorship. There was little in them to lift me. A whole page was given over every week to the dismal humors of M. Quad — Mr. Bowser, the Limekiln Club, the *Arizona Kicker*, Major Crowfoot, and so on. Quad was an old-time printer whose actual name was Charles B. Lewis. He was the last of the long line of American newspaper humorists which began with Seba Smith (Major Jack Downing), and ran through H. W. Shaw (Josh Billings), D. R. Locke (Petroleum V. Nasby) and C. F. Browne (Artemus Ward) to Bill Nye and Bob Burdette. George Ade and Finley Peter Dunne were already blazing new paths in Chicago, but as yet they were not syndicated, and I had to do without them. I paid Quad $5 a week for his page, which included the matrices for four or five illustrations. He was already an old man, and from his home in Brooklyn he farmed out his work to various bright young reporters in New York. All of his features followed precise patterns, and it was child's play to write them.

Another stand-by of the *Sunday Herald* — and of scores of other Sunday papers — was the weekly travel article of Frank G. Carpenter. He was the Marco Polo of his generation, and had been roving the world since 1881. The stuff that he sent back from such places as Tierra del Fuego, Lapland and Cochin-China was excessively dull, and the photographs that came with it made engravers weep, but there was a superstition on the

Herald that the customers liked travel articles, and so I had to print him. One day a young man walked into the office with the news that he was barging into the trade in competition with Carpenter. He had with him, and exhibited, some specimens of his art: they had to do, as I recall, with South America. They were so much better than Carpenter's that I took on this newcomer at once. His name was Frederic J. Haskin, and he came from Quincy, Ill. He demanded $10 a week, whereas Carpenter had got but $5, but I was so glad to get rid of Carpenter that I strained my budget to pay it. Haskin continued to do his own traveling and writing for some years thereafter, but then he began to give over most of his time to selling his stuff, and hired assistants to fetch it in. He was a superb salesman, and at his peak was probably the most successful syndicate man in America, with a weekly foreign letter, a daily article from Washington, and a questions-and-answers service that still exists. He began to publish books for the one-book-a-year trade in 1911, with such titles as " The American Government," " The Panama Canal " and " 10,000 Answers to Questions," and ran up such sales that the regular publishers of the country were staggered. I got to know him very well, and every time he dropped off in Baltimore we gave over the evening to drinking Pilsner and laughing at the human race. His journalistic bee-hive in Washington turned out some notable graduates, for example, Louis Brownlow, the expert on municipal government, and Harvey Fergusson, the novelist.

My own writing for the *Sunday Herald* was pretty well confined to the theatre pages : I had too many troubles to do much else. Those pages, as such things ran in that era, were not bad. I devoted them to plays rather than to actors, and made a point of giving some account of every new drama of any importance that reached the stage, whether in this country or Europe. Not many that were worth describing came along, and I was often reduced to wasting space on trash, but now and then a Shaw or a Hauptmann stepped up to the bat for me, and I was happy. The frenzied encomiums on actors that poured in from press-agents I cut down to brief paragraphs and printed literally, with a heading reading " What the Press-Agents Say." There was a weekly letter about stage doings in New York by Charles Henry Meltzer, who had been dramatic critic for the New York *Herald* and *World* and one of the associates of James Huneker on *M'lle New York*. My main effort, outside the theatre pages, was devoted to reforming the archaic typography of the Sunday paper, and trying to get rid of its ancient features. As I have said, I succeeded with Carpenter but failed with M. Quad. One of its worst relics of a more innocent day was a full page of fraternal order news — supplied free by the secretaries of the various lodges, but so badly written that copy-reading it was a heavy chore. The theory in the office was that this balderdash made circulation — that all the joiners of the town searched it every Sunday morning for their own names. This seemed to me to be bad reasoning, for any given joiner was bound to be disappointed nine Sundays out of ten. One Sunday I quietly dropped the page — and not a single protest came in.

Carter quit as managing editor at the end of 1902 and was succeeded by Lynn R. Meekins, of whom a great deal will be heard in Chapters XIX and XX. Meekins, after spending a couple of weeks surveying the office, decided that the city-room, since Max Ways's time, had been going downhill. This was something that was palpable to the meanest understanding, and no one knew it better than I, who had emerged from the place only a little while before. A good many of the more competent men of Ways's days had disappeared, and their places had been taken by third-, fourth- and fifth-raters. That they wrote bad stuff was not unnatural, but that it got into the paper was really shocking. I well recall my writhing discomfort over some of it. When, in the Autumn of 1901, the immortal McKinley was done to death by one of Hitler's agents, and his remains were dragged through Baltimore on their way to Washington, the following paragraph was actually printed in a *news* story:

In the silent masonry of men's souls all over this fair land of ours you hold a place today with Washington and Lincoln — a place no power can plead away — a place God-given by right of honor and justice, peace and equity, faith and hope. Vale McKinley!

This drivel, it appears, was highly esteemed by the city editor of the time. Carter should have killed it, but Carter was but little interested in the news department, and seldom read the proofs that reached his desk every night. Meekins was much more attentive, and during his first month he got rid of several of the worst word-painters. But a lot of muck remained, and he decided finally to put in a new city editor. When he offered the job to me I was really astonished, and, what is more, considerably alarmed. It was, to be sure, a step up that must have flattered any youngster of twenty-three, but I knew that reorganizing the staff would be a difficult job, and I was in fear that I'd have special difficulties with some of the older men, several of whom, at one time or another, had been my superiors. But Meekins was optimistic, and my fear turned out to be without ground. With one or two exceptions, all the old-timers gave me hearty support, and at Meekins's suggestion I got rid of the worst of the rag-tag and bob-tail by firing a whole platoon of them on my first day at the city-desk.

This was wise surgery, but it left the staff much depleted, and my job for a while was less that of a city editor than that of a rewrite man. In fact, I usually put in all my time from 9 p.m. onward rewriting leads, leaving my assistant, Joe Callahan, to run the desk. Meekins was pleased with the improvement in the paper, and especially with the disappearance of fustian and hooey, but when he discovered what I was doing he prohibited it, and ordered me to stick to my proper duties. My model and idol, in those days, was the New York *Sun*, and I made desperate efforts to bring the *Herald* up to its standard of good writing. This, of course, was impossible, for there were no such reporters in Baltimore as those who adorned the *Sun*, but nevertheless some progress was made, and after the staff had been strengthened with a few good men the *Herald* began to shine. To this day, in fact, no American provincial paper that I can recall has ever been so briskly written. We were often beaten on news by the Baltimore *Sunpaper*, but our bright young men wrote rings around it every day.

I soon found, as every young city editor must find, that Sunday night brings the zero hour of the week. There is, ordinarily, very little news stirring, and that little tends to be a great deal less than exhilarating. Everything really interesting and instructive falls off on Sunday, from murders to dog-fights. The courts, the City Hall, and a dozen other principal sources of news are closed, and the public orgies of the day are of a predom-

inantly chaste and diuretic character.[2] That was
a red-letter Sunday, in 1903, when news came in
that a colored lodge of Odd Fellows, excursioning
on the Chesapeake in a barge towed by a tug, had
been run down by a banana boat, and another when
a wild man was reported loose in the woods over
Baltimore's northern city-line, with every dog
barking for miles around, and all women and children locked up. I got special delight out of the
wild man, for I had invented him myself, and no
one else knew that he was imaginary save Tom
Dempsey, an old-time police lieutenant, who had
kindly helped me with the job. The other cops took
him quite seriously, and hunted him with loud
shouts and the frequent discharge of their pistols.
Before the day was over they had roped and
brought in at least a dozen poor bums, and put
them through very stiff workouts in the back room.
When Monday dawned, and Baltimore resumed its
usual carnalities, the wild man was forgotten, but
Dempsey and I revived him the next Sunday, and
so every week for a month following. The story
was spoiled at last when an alarmed magistrate, believing the bogus evidence offered by the cops
against a half-wit stranger that they had collared,

[2] In these days, of course, there is always a heavy grist of
fatal automobile accidents, but it is seldom that anyone of any
importance is killed. Politicians have learned to reserve their
radio crooning and other prophesying for Sunday nights, but
their blather commonly comes by wire, and thus does not help
city editors.

sentenced him to six months in the House of Correction.

I discovered one day that what would now be called an Open Forum was in operation on Sunday afternoons in a hall over a West Baltimore livery-stable, and assigned a reporter without too much conscience to have a look. He came back with a swell story about a riotous debate between a Single Taxer and a Socialist, with the Socialist pulling a butcher-knife and the Single Taxer leaping out of a window. The two came in the next day to protest that the matter had been exaggerated, but I nevertheless continued the same reporter on the job, and in a little while he had peopled the Open Forum with a whole stock company of fantastic characters, some of them still remembered in Baltimore. His imagination was of high octane content, but his literary style ran to long and tortured sentences. I took over the burden of reading copy on him, and usually managed to translate him into reasonably clear English. Unhappily, I eventually lost him, for his writing was so bad that it got him a job as editorial writer on another paper. His efforts, while he lasted, reduced the whole Open Forum movement in Baltimore to the level of barroom humor, and to this day no one there cares what is said or advocated by the orators who rant and roar in such quarters. They can argue for Communism all they please, or even for cannibalism, adultery or kidnaping. The very cops listen placidly.

For a while this sort of thing entertained me pleasantly, but in the end it began to bore me. I was, I suspect, a bad city editor. My interest in what is called spot news had begun to wither after I was graduated from police reporting myself, and I was now chiefly intent on making the *Herald* better written. Any reporter who could write reasonably well seemed a good one to me, and any one who couldn't a mutt. This judgment could be defended like any other, but there was also a good deal to be said against it. I took a number of long chances with stories chiefly fanciful, but curiously enough, picked up no libel suits save with those that were substantially true. The worst of these litigations (which always alarm a newspaper office, however easy their defense may look) was launched by a lady who, according to the cops, was a common prostitute. She was the widow of an Italian who had also left another widow, and this other one had later married a Chinaman. One night Widow No. 1 was jugged for street-walking, and the cops mistook her for Widow No. 2. When the *Herald* reported the next morning, relying on their dope, that she was the Chinaman's wife she instructed her solicitor to enter suit. We thought we had her, for dozens of cops volunteered to testify that she was free of both the white and black races, and hence

139

had no reputation to lose, but the judge ruled out all this testimony on the ground that it had nothing to do with our false and foul allegation that she had married a Chinaman. Even a street-walker, he said, might object to that, at least in the eye of the law. We seemed to be lost, but at the last minute the lady's solicitor, not content to let well enough alone, rose up to address the jury. Within two minutes his eloquent description of her mental anguish had the twelve jurymen snickering, and in five minutes they were howling, along with the learned judge. Our own lawyer kept silent, and the jury gave us a verdict without leaving the box.

Not infrequently the long hours and endless vexations of my job worked me down so far that I was in a state bordering on paranoia. The *Herald* office, by this time, had a complete outfit of telephones, and mine rang an average of once a minute. I had to keep track of the comings and goings of thirty men, some of them with a high talent for disappearing. It was a formidable business, when a big fire broke out or a nice murder was announced, to round up enough of them to cover it, and once they got out of sight it was quite as harassing to recover them. Very often, at the end of a long afternoon, I'd sneak out of the office for a little peace, and let it sweat and fester on its own. Sometimes I would go to a French restaurant a few blocks away, where a slow but sound meal was to be had for sixty cents, and the proprietor (who was also the chef) turned up a new wife (who was also the cashier) every month. That refuge was spoiled one night when two of these wives had it out with crockery just as I was about to sit down to a plate of onion soup. I then took to making quiet round trips to Washington, and dining on the train. In those days every city editor had a pocketful of annual passes: I had them myself, in fact, on every railroad east of St. Louis or north of Atlanta, and also on all the coastwise steam-packets. The dining-car dinners I thus engulfed were seldom very appetizing, but it was refreshing to escape from the city-room for a while and rest my eyes on the frowsy wilderness that runs between Baltimore and Washington. When I saw a yap at a cross-roads, waiting on his mule for the train to pass, I forgot the hookworms and other parasites at work upon his liver and lights, and almost envied him.

But despite all these woes I still had a reasonably pleasant time, and my leisure, though scanty, was at least more than I had enjoyed as a reporter. One of its fruits was a sharp revival of my interest in music. Carter had given me a start in that direction, and now I was helped on by the learned conversation of our music critic, Owst, who was an abyss of thorough-bass, and set me to studying a textbook of that science; by daily contact with Lew Schaefer, one of the reporters, who devoted his own leisure to writing piano pieces for children; and, above all, by the untutored but very real enthusiasm of my assistant, Joe Callahan. Joe was perhaps the worst violinist who ever lived; in fact, his technic went but little beyond the open strings; but he knew a great many musicians, and brought me into contact with them. It was through him that I met Fred Gottlieb, a rich brewer who was also an amateur flautist, and Al Hildebrandt, a violin-dealer by trade who played the cello for the fun of it, and remained one of my warmest friends to the end of his days. There were also Isidor Goodman, the night editor, who had once played the flute in a circus band, and Emanuel Daniel, assistant sporting editor, who passed in the office under the nickname of Schmool, and was a violinist. Under Joe's conniving, Schmool, Al and I took to playing trios, and in a little while other amateurs joined us, and then a few professionals, and by 1904 we had a club meeting regularly. It exists to the present day, and I never miss one of its Saturday night sessions when I am in Baltimore. I am now the only survivor of its original members. Goodman never belonged to it, but he and I often played together, for he had a girl who was a singer, and he liked to play flute obbligatos to her singing, while I did the piano accompaniment. For these refined soirées we commonly borrowed a small studio in a piano-dealer's establishment, a block from the *Herald* office. There was never any audience, for Goodman believed that his technic had degenerated since his circus days, and was shy of criticism. As for me, I banged away innocently, and often drowned out both the poor girl's voice and her admirer's tootling.

Goodman had an elder brother named Al who was the *Herald's* political reporter. He had a bald head and a Van Dyke beard and was old enough to be my father, but we got on very well, and he taught me a great deal about the science of politics as he had observed it. It was his theory that all reformers were either frauds or idiots, and that some of them were both. He believed that practical politicians, taking one with another, made the safest and most competent public officials, if only because they were intelligent. He granted somewhat grudgingly that there were occasional thieves among them, but he argued that their worst corruptions were cheaper to the taxpayer than the insane wastes of the uplift. It was from him that I first heard all the familiar maxims of American statecraft, for example, " In politics a man must learn to rise *above* principle," and " When the water reaches the upper deck follow the rats." Al took me to my first pair of national conventions — those of 1904. In theory I was his superior officer, but I was glad to go as his legman, for he knew all the politicians, high and low, and was full of illuminating confidences about them. I recall his telling me in St. Louis that William Jennings Bryan, though a teetotaler, was a glutton, and predicting that he would eat himself to death. This prophecy was a long time coming true, but after twenty-two years it came true at last.

Al always wrote a long political disquisition for the Sunday *Herald*, and usually composed it in the city-room on Saturday afternoon, when there was comparative quiet there. He looked upon the type-writer as a new-fangled absurdity, and always wrote by hand. Ever and anon he would pause in his work, slap his bald head, clear his throat, and deliver himself of a soliloquy of his own composition. It began as follows:

Yes, my belovéd bullpups: it was not always thus. So his arse hit the ceiling with great éclat, and the little birds sang hallelujah.

This went on for a minute or two, and then rounded up with a quotation from " Barbara Frietchie ":

" Strike, if you must, this old gray head,
But spare your country's flag," she said.

Once a female reporter, overhearing this ritual, complained to me that it was painful to her pruderies. I invited her to do her work thereafter in the press-room, for I admired Al, and greatly enjoyed his observations, however vulgar. He and his brother Isidor had nicknames for all the office boys, usually borrowed from the Yiddish nomenclature, and often indecent. They also had nicknames for most of the reporters and editors. I daresay they

144

had one for me, too, and maybe a blistering one, but if so I never heard it. City editors, in those days, were addressed familiarly by their given names by all save the youngest reporters, but even in those days city editors were treated a bit tenderly.

The supreme climax and boiling point of my service in that office I reserve for Chapter XIX.

IX

THREE

MANAGING EDITORS

In the days of which I write the chief editorial dignitary on every American daily paper was called the managing editor, and his jurisdiction extended, not only over all the news departments, but also over the editorial page. He was himself, in fact, the chief editorial writer, and on most papers his only help in that line came from two or three ancient hulks who were unfit for any better duty — copy-readers promoted from the city-room to get rid of them, alcoholic writers of local histories and forgotten novels, former managing editors who had come to grief on other papers, and a miscellany of decayed lawyers, college professors and clergymen with whispered pasts. Some of these botches of God were pleasant enough fellows, and a few even showed a certain grasp of elemental English, but taking one with another they were held in disdain by the reporters, and it was almost unheard of for one of them to be promoted to a better job. Everyone believed as an axiom that they lifted four-fifths of their editorials from other papers, and most authorities held that they bitched them in the lifting. If anyone in the city-room had ever spoken of an editorial in his own paper as cogent and illuminating he would have been set down as a jackass for admiring it and as a kind of traitor to honest journalism for reading it at all. No editorial writer was ever applied to for a loan, or invited to an office booze-party.

But the managing editor, though he also wrote editorials, escaped the infamy of the caste, no doubt because he was mainly concerned with news, and usually emanated from the news department himself. He was, indeed, the chief hero of all the younger reporters, even when they denounced him for overworking and underpaying them, and they tried to model their mien and metaphysic on his — that is, provided he were not, by an office calamity, a teetotaler or an opponent of smoking. Myths about him were always in circulation, some of them based upon actual feats of professional or other derring-do, but most of them purely imaginary. Colonel A. B. Cunningham, managing editor of the *Herald* when I joined its staff in 1899, was generally depicted, by office gossip, as a very truculent and even bloodthirsty man, with a long record of

carnage behind him. His career in the Confederate
Army was assimilated to those of Jeb Stuart, J. S.
Mosby and Joe Wheeler, and it was believed that
he had refused to come in after Appomattox, but
chosen rather to flee to Egypt, where he gradually
cooled himself off by slaughtering dervishes. He
had worked as a reporter on the St. Louis *Post-
Dispatch* under the celebrated John Albert Cockerill, and out of the fact developed a legend that he
had once fought a duel with Cockerill, with bowie
knives as weapons.

The colonel's aspect gave a certain amount of
support to his reputation, for he was tall, well-
built and of military bearing, had flashing black
eyes under heavy brows, and wore his wavy, coal-
black hair brushed back from his forehead. His
head, in fact, was a fine one, and his smooth-shaven
face was not unhandsome. But he was actually a
much milder man than his lieges believed, and it
was only when he was in his cups that he made any
noise in the office. The facts about him came out in
1906, when he reached the dignity of inclusion in
" Who's Who in America." He was a native, it
appeared, of Minden, a small town in northwestern
Louisiana, just under the Arkansas line, and he
was less than fifteen years old when the Civil War
began. But despite his tender years he enlisted in
the Eighteenth Louisiana Infantry, and after that,
in succession, in the Fifth Texas Cavalry and Mc-
Nelly's Scouts, and fought doggedly until the end

of the war. After Appomattox he put in a few years at flag-stop colleges in Louisiana, and then, in 1874, he was offered a commission in the Egyptian Army, which was being reorganized on a grandiose scale by the spendthrift Ismail. Many other ex-Confederates received similar offers, and some actually went to Egypt, but Cunningham apparently never made the trip, though he kept his title of colonel (*bey*) for the rest of his life. It was, in its way, a kind of gilding of the lily, for all Southern editors in that era were colonels by brevet, and many of them, especially in the smaller towns, are so to this day. When I became managing editor of the *Herald* myself, in 1905, I was usually so addressed in communications from confrères below the Potomac.

The colonel seldom showed himself in the cityroom, save to stalk through it, but he knew all the reporters by name, and sometimes joined in their extramural activities. At the time of the first election I ever helped to cover there was a dollar pool in the office on the majority of the winning candidate, and the colonel won it. It amounted to $50 or $60, and he blew in the money royally on a midnight supper to the staff. Toward the end of the party, which was large and loud, someone remembered that the annual ball of the Nonpareil Social Club was going on in a shabby hall near the waterfront, and it was resolved to look in. The Nonpareil was one of two rival organizations of Balti-

more harlots, or, perhaps more accurately, of their
male parasites and protectors, and its functions
were always attended by large delegations of whiskey drummers, brewery collectors, professional
bondsmen, minor court officials, and cops in mufti.
By the time we got to the hall it was pretty late,
and the festivities on the floor were abating, but the
colonel revived them by taking a seat in the front
row of the gallery, and heaving handfuls of small
silver overboard. No less than three times he had
$10 bills changed into dimes, and every time he
went into action all the waiters on the floor dropped
their trays and began to scramble for the money.
The third time a committee consisting of two distinguished madames and a deputy sheriff came up
to the gallery to protest. They said the honor of
his presence was appreciated, but that his largess
was incommoding the service of drinks and wreck-
ing the ball. He professed to be offended, and
threatened to denounce the affair in a *Herald* editorial as snobbish and anti-social, but he was only
having his joke, and in a little while he gave the
signal for us to withdraw. On the street outside,
stimulated by the dawn, he lined us up along the
curbstone, and gave the signal for one of those
combats in uresis which festive males of *Homo
sapiens* have been carrying on since the days of
Abraham. It was won easily by a young reporter
with powerful reflexes, whose name sounded something like Macon.

When the rival organization, the Rogers Pleasure Social, gave a ball a few weeks later, it sent a special committee to the *Herald* office to invite the colonel and his suite, but he said he had had enough of sexual society for a while, and refused to come. The rest of us, however, went in strength, and had the pleasure of witnessing a battle with beer bottles between two madames. Both were blooded, and the cops made a great pother of dragging them apart and carting them to hospital. Many of the more nefarious political clubs of the town gave somewhat similar parties, and we were usually invited. I remember one especially, for it was arranged in layers, with the wives and daughters of the ward heelers entertained on the second floor and the fancy women on the third. The former danced to a five-piece orchestra and the latter to a hand-organ. When we reporters arrived at the street door and made ourselves known we were ushered at once to the third floor.

The colonel had only contempt for the public attentions that pursue newspaper editors. He never went to a banquet if he could help it, and never signed manifestoes or sat on committees. The only public office he ever accepted was membership on the Baltimore School Board, which was unpaid. This was in 1901 or thereabout, and an effort was being made at the time to rid the Baltimore schools of the dirt pedagogy that had prevailed in them since colonial times, and to substitute the new wizardries from Teachers College, Columbia. The president of the board was a local corporation lawyer of the highest elegance, and one of the members was Dr. Daniel Coit Gilman, president of the Johns Hopkins University. I was assigned to cover the meetings for the *Herald* and commonly returned from them with the colonel, riding on the rear platform of a trolley-car. He never made any suggestions about the way the story was to be written, but in the confidence of a smoke together he often thought aloud about his fellow-members, most of whom he put in the debased class of uplifters. One evening he asked me if I had taken notice of one who spoke habitually in despairing tones, wore a long-tailed coat, and looked the perfect Christian philanthropist. " That poor eunuch," he said, " claims to be the father of five or six children. Turn your mind to the physiology of mammalian reproduction, and see if you can imagine it." I had to confess that I couldn't.

When it came to salaries the colonel was excessively hard-boiled, for the *Herald,* in those days, was poor compared to the *Sun* and *News:* even his own pay, as I learned on becoming managing editor myself and snooping through the books, was never more than $90 a week. But he stuck to his men when they got into trouble, and it was on such occasions that his Southern fire was oftenest manifested. I well recall a case in point, for I was a figure in it. It came in the first years of the century, when not only the public schools, but also all the other municipal departments of Baltmore, including even the police force, were in the clutches of primeval New Dealers. Presently the poor cops had a new and terrifying master — a retired Army captain with a walrus moustache who had been sitting for years in the window of the Athenaeum Club in Charles street, glaring at the passers-by. His name was Hamilton, and he was the perfect model of the *Rittmeister* of tradition — stiff, vain, boorish and stupid. He set the cops to saluting on all occasions, ordered the old ones to train off their bay-windows, and put the whole unhappy outfit to drilling in the hot sun.

These reforms made for news, but getting it was something else again. When I was assigned to headquarters, and made my first call at the new chief's office, he let me stand for at least ten minutes while he busied himself with the papers on his desk. The second day I stood for fifteen minutes, and the third day for twenty minutes, and when the old boy looked up at last he would bark as if I had been an insurance agent or a collector for the orphans. After that I kept out of his office, and my information about his doings was derived from cops who were as friendly to newspaper reporters as they were hostile to their new commander. The inevitable result was that the *Herald* printed some stories that annoyed him, and in a little while he wrote a letter to the colonel, complaining that I never came near his office and that my reports of his doings were faked. This was a serious charge and the colonel ordered me up for trial the next morning. My defense was brief: I simply told the truth. The colonel was not long in reaching his verdict. " Go back to that goddam son-of-a-bitch," he roared, " and tell him with my compliments that a *Herald* reporter kisses *no* man's arse." I relayed this communiqué to Hamilton through one of his stooges, and he was polite enough thereafter. Before long he had got the cops into such a mess that he had to be kicked out, and they returned joyously to Bach.

When the *Herald* was sold to Wesley M. Oler, a rich Baltimorean who had made his money in the ice business and eventually rose to be president of the American Ice Company, the colonel's position became very uncomfortable, for Oler was a Republican and wanted to use the paper to promote his political aspirations, which were wide and deep. The colonel, of course, was a Democrat. After a series of squabbles he quit his job and started an afternoon paper of his own, but it blew up quickly, and he became the Baltimore agent of the Associated Press.[1] His successor was Robert I. Carter, who had been recommended to Oler by the Tafts of Cincinnati, where he had worked on the *Times-*

[1] He died in Baltimore in 1915. Born in 1846, he was 54 years old in 1900, but to us young reporters he seemed a patriarch.

Star and assisted in launching William Howard of
that ilk as a statesman. On all imaginable counts
he was at the opposite pole from the colonel. A
native of Massachusetts and a graduate of Harvard, with a game leg, a conservative paunch and
a red Van Dyke beard, he looked the college pro-
fessor far more than the newspaper editor, and in
all his tastes, methods of work, theories of journalism and habits of mind he differed abysmally from
his predecessor. At the start the boys in the *Herald*
office hardly knew what to make of him, for it was
quickly bruited about that he could speak seven
(soon lifted to seventeen) languages, and he
alarmed everybody on his second night by showing
up in a dinner coat. But it soon became apparent
that he was anything but a dilettante, and when
he fired several old-timers, ordered some raises in
salaries, and put a rambunctious female reporter
in her place, office opinion began to swing toward
him, and the usual legends about him were hatched.
One was to the effect that he had killed a man in
Cincinnati, and another accounted for his game
leg by a fall off a fire-escape leading down from the
boudoir of a rich brewer's beautiful fourth wife.
He was reputed to be wealthy himself, and there
were two theories about the origin of his hoard:
one being that he was an heir of the Carter's Ink
fortune and the other that he was an heir of the
Carter's Little Liver Pills fortune.

My own relations with him have been described

more or less in Chapter VII. He was a highly civilized and very charming man, and his influence upon me at a time when I was in some danger of yielding to the Philistinism which then dominated Baltimore journalism was powerful and all to the good. He made it plain to me, and to others, that it was quite possible to be a good newspaper man, and still cherish some pretense to decent tastes. His own eager interest in the fine arts, and especially in music and the drama, was contagious, but he was as far from being priggish as the old colonel himself. On the contrary, he was a very amiable and expansive fellow, fond of good eating and drinking, and tolerant of the so-called Bohemianism of the city-room, though he kept aloof from it himself. He fired the old-timers, not primarily because they were boozers, but because they were booze-grafters, and hence disgraceful to the paper.

The job he had taken on was not an easy one, for the departure of Cunningham, followed soon by that of Max Ways, and then by that of Nachman, the business manager, had left the *Herald* organization crippled and demoralized. Carter tried out several new city editors in succession, but they fell very far short of Ways. He was burdened with editorial writers even worse than usual, and was reduced at one time to inviting members of the city staff to contribute volunteer editorials. But his most severe headaches came from above, not below. Oler was a poor substitute for William Howard

Taft, though he had the same itch to shine in statecraft. He was a tall, thin, dour Methodist with a funereal black beard, and never got to first base in politics, though he once collared a great deal of notice (at least in his own paper) by inducing Theodore Roosevelt, then President, to ride over from Washington to visit him in his suburban mansion. Roosevelt, who made the trip on horseback, followed by a squad of sweating Army officers, let it be known that Oler was a man of astounding abilities and would make a superb United States Senator, but no one else ever believed it. To replace the smart and competent Nachman as business manager he brought in a Canadian named Peard — a majestic and singularly handsome fellow with no more capacity for the job than a police sergeant. So the *Herald* gradually got into difficulties, and Carter's hard work went for nothing. He modernized the typography of the paper, reformed some of its archaic Southern practises, and brought in a few good men, but in the end he had to confess failure. After two years and two months of it he resigned in January, 1903, and was succeeded by Lynn R. Meekins.[2]

2 Carter joined the New York *Herald* after leaving Baltimore, and became editor of its Paris edition and one of the confidential men of James Gordon Bennett. He had traveled very widely as a young man and now traveled even more. I encountered him occasionally in New York after he left Baltimore, but eventually lost sight of him. He disappeared from Who's Who in America after the 1912–13 edition. He was 32 years old when he came to the *Herald* in Baltimore.

Of the three managing editors that I sat under on the *Herald* Meekins was the most competent, and by long odds, but he came into the office carrying several handicaps, and it took him some time to get rid of them; indeed, it was not until the great Baltimore fire of 1904 brought out his quick resourcefulness and high capacity for command that he was generally accepted in the office. His first handicap was that he had got most of his training on the Baltimore *American*, a rival that was not even given the flattery of fear, but simply held in contempt. His second was that he had spent most of his seventeen years there writing editorials — a trade, as I have said, that no reporter respected. His third, and heaviest, was that he was reported to be a Methodist, and what is worse, a Methodist of the so-called Methodist Protestant sub-sect, which, even in 1903, was already whooping up Prohibition. When his membership in this infamous outfit was confirmed there was something close to moral indignation in the office, and one of the artists actually announced that, provided he could find a better job elsewhere, he would resign in protest.

Nor did Meekins's first tour of inspection reassure the brethren, for he turned out to be a slight, clerical-looking fellow wearing a small gray moustache and scholarly spectacles, with a voice that never arose to the barks and snarls proper to a managing editor. But though the legend of his

anti-social heresies persisted for a year, it was
soon apparent to the more judicious that he was
anything but a milksop. On the contrary, he
turned out to be bold and even pugnacious, and in
a little while he was carrying on a revolt against
Peard's ineptitudes downstairs, and getting rid of
a lot of dead wood in the editorial rooms. My own
inclination was to see something in him, for he
had two novels behind him and was a frequent con-
tributor to *Harper's Magazine;* and that inclination was converted into an active prejudice pro
when he called me into his office one day and told
me that my salary as Sunday editor was to be increased $5 a week. This was the first time since I
had joined the *Herald* that I had ever got a raise
without first being offered a better job elsewhere,
and the miracle naturally filled me with amiable
sentiments. Nor was my delight diminished when
he told me that I needed better help in my job, and
ordered me to find a couple of likely young aides,
male or female. What he had to say about the Sunday edition, some of it favorable but most of it
critical, was searching and sensible, and I soon discovered that he knew more about such things than
anyone else in the office. This, I must confess,
seemed incredible in an editorial writer — until
presently I learned that, in the interval between
writing editorials for the *American* and coming to
the *Herald,* he had been the first managing editor
of the *Saturday Evening Post,* then just started

159

on its opulent career of fostering the national letters.

But the fact remained that Meekins, compared to Cunningham or even to Carter, was a subdued and highly respectable fellow, and that life in the *Herald* office began to lose something of its old wild glitter. He was not, it soon appeared, an actual Prohibitionist, but he had a low opinion of the more alcoholic journalists of the era, and began to ease them out one by one. The *Herald* office thus became much more efficient than it had ever been before, but it ceased to be as merry as it once was, and if the men got more money they enjoyed less recreation, as recreation was then understood. We had another Methodist in the office, a reporter named Stockbridge, but he was so pleasant a fellow that no one held it against him, though we showed our dissent from his superstitions by giving him the satirical title of Bishop. When, in July, 1903, Pope Leo XIII died, and the cardinals began hustling to Rome to elect his successor, an office wag put the following notice on the city-room bulletin-board:

FOR POPE:

The Right Rev. Jason Stockbridge, D.D.,
Bishop of Sodom and Gomorrah *in partibus infidelium*
Subject to the Democratic primaries

This jocosity, though it lay snugly within the traditional *Herald* pattern of office humor, outraged Meekins, and he not only ordered it removed at once but went through the forms of an investigation that lasted for two weeks. While his inquiries were going on I trembled lest he accuse some innocent member of the staff, and so force me to step up and confess the truth, which was that I had done the deed myself. But the investigation frittered out without an indictment, and it was years later, after the *Herald* had been long buried, and forgotten by all save its alumni, that Meekins told me he had recognized my literary style at once. His failure to accuse me was revelatory of his peculiar character: he was fundamentally a somewhat prissy fellow, but he always refrained from wreaking his prissiness on others. Until his professional exploits at the time of the fire of 1904 won him unanimous acceptance at last, he remained a suspicious person to most of the reporters, for it was still a cardinal article of office doctrine that a Methodist (despite the glaring contrary example of Bishop Stockbridge) was necessarily and *ipso facto* a devious, inimical and mean fellow, bent only on afflicting and injuring the human race. But Meekins was constantly doing things that made that easy formula untenable, and the ground was thus gradually preparing for his elevation to respect and esteem in 1904. If there had never been any fire it might have been delayed, and without question it would have stopped short of canonization, but certainly it would have come.

Meekins had been born in a small village on the

Eastern Shore of Maryland, where Yahweh remains a threatening character to this day, and if he kept some of the theological naïveté of his native wildwood, he also showed a good deal of country humor. He took the horrible alarms and vicissitudes of newspaper life without too much seriousness, and was full of sharp judgments of men and events. He viewed editorial writers much as reporters viewed them, though he had been one for so many years himself, and at a later period, when he resumed the shroud of the craft in the service of Hearst, he cackled over its futilities every time we met. It was his theory that no editorial that showed genuine sense was fit to print, or, indeed, could be printed without danger. He could write very good ones on occasion, for he had a clear mind and a first-rate English style, but he got more fun, I am sure, out of writing the bad ones — for example, arguments in favor of new parks and a reformed police force, and obituary encomiums of dead local worthies, nine-tenths of whom he knew personally to be either idiots or scoundrels. The Hearst paper he worked for was the heir of both his first love, the Baltimore *American,* and the Baltimore *News.* Its leading editorials were mainly canned goods from the New York headquarters of the chain; his job was simply to keep the home fires burning. A conservative by instinct, he was amused rather than outraged by the exuberance of the Hearst typography, and used to defend it wryly on the ground that it at least enabled him to fill a lot of space at small expense of labor.

As an author himself he took a great deal of interest in my own literary strivings. His advice in that department was always sound, and he was ever ready with it. He knew most of the American literati of the Howells generation, and was full of illuminating anecdotes about them. His own writings were in their manner, but he was very hospitable to the newcomers who finally unhorsed them, and he did a great deal of miscellaneous reading, even in his busiest days as managing editor of the uremic *Herald*, and, later, as its publisher. Unlike Carter, he had no appetite for music and very little for the theatre, but his knowledge of books was enormous, and he set me to reading many a tome that I might have missed otherwise. I suspect that it was largely his influence that caused me to resolve, when the *Herald* finally went down, to subordinate executive work, during the rest of my days, to writing. In all probability he lived to regret that he had not done so himself.[3]

3 Meekins died in 1933 in London, where his only son was commercial attaché of the American embassy.

X

SLAVES OF

BEAUTY

IT was not until I became Sunday editor that I had any official relations with the fantastic Crocodilidæ known as newspaper artists, but I had naturally encountered a number of them in my days as a reporter. The first one I ever saw in the flesh, so far as I can recall, was an Irishman wearing a seedy checked suit, a purple Windsor tie, a malacca stick, and a *boutonnière* consisting of two pink rosebuds fastened together with tinfoil. This was in a saloon near the *Herald* office in the year 1899, and I remember saying to myself that he certainly looked the part. It appeared at once that he also acted it, for when the bartender hinted that the price of beer was still five cents a glass, cash on delivery, the artist first snuffled up what remained of the foam in his schooner, and then replied calmly that it was to be charged to his account. I was still, in those days, a cub reporter, and full of an innocent delight in the wonders of the world. The decaying veteran at my side had invited me out, as he put it, to introduce me to society, and while he did the introducing I bought the beer. He now nudged me, and whispered romantically that the artist had spent his last ten cents for the *boutonnière:* it had been bought, it appeared, of a street vendor in front of police headquarters — a one-armed man who was reputed to get his stock by raiding colored graveyards by night. This vendor trusted no one below the rank of a police lieutenant, so the rosebuds had to be paid for, but bartenders showed more confidence in humanity. After the artist had filled his pockets with pretzels and stalked out grandly, flirting his malacca stick in the manner of James A. McNeill Whistler, the old-timer explained that he was honorable above the common, and always paid his reckonings in the long run. "Whenever," I was informed, "some woman with money gets stuck on him, or he sells a couple of comics to a syndicate, he goes around town settling up. Once I saw him lay out $17 in one night. He had to beat it from England in a cattle-boat. There was a rich Jewish duke packing a gun for him."

I never saw this marvel again, for a few days later he was shanghaied on the Baltimore water-

front, and when, after a couple of months of bitter
Winter weather down Chesapeake Bay, he escaped
from the oyster fleet by legging it over the ice, he
made tracks for Canada and the protection of the
Union Jack, leaving more than one bartender to
mourn him. But in the course of the next half
dozen years, first as Sunday editor, then as city
editor, and finally in the austere misery of managing editor, I made acquaintance with many other
artists, and acquired a lot of unpleasant information about their habits and customs. They ranged
from presumably respectable married men with
families (sometimes, indeed, with two families)
down to wastrels who floated in from points South
or West, remained only long enough to lift an overcoat and two or three bottles of Higgins's drawing
ink, and then vanished as mysteriously as they had
come. A few of them even neglected to draw their
pay — always to the indignation of the office
cashier, who had to carry a small and incredible
overage on his books until he got up nerve enough
to buy the city editor a couple of drinks, and so
discharge his debt for theatre passes. But whatever the differences marking off these jitney
Dürers into phyla and species, they all had certain
traits in common, mostly productive of indignation
in editors. Each and every one of them looked
down his nose at the literati of journalism, and
laughed at them as Philistines almost comparable
to bartenders or policemen. One and all had an al-

most supernatural talent for getting out of the
way when fire broke out in a medical college or
orphan asylum, and there were loud yells for illus-
trative art. And so far as I can recall, there was
never one who failed, soon or late, to sneak something scandalous into a picture at the last moment,
to the delight the next morning of every soul in
town save what we then called the Moral Element.

I write, of course, of an era long past and by
most persons forgotten, and I have no doubt that
artists are now much changed, whether on newspapers or off. Some time ago a man in charge of
the art department of a great metropolitan daily
told me that fully a third of his men read the
Nation, and that many of the rest had joined the
C.I.O. and were actually paying their dues. He
even alleged that there were two teetotalers among
them, not to mention a theosophist. In my time
nothing of the sort was heard of. The artists of
that day were all careless and carnal fellows, with
no interest in their souls and no sense of social responsibility. Their *beau idéal* was still the Rodolfo
of " La Bohème," and if not Rodolfo, then some
salient whiskey drummer, burlesque manager or
other Elk; for the contemporaneous Roosevelts,
Willkies, Hulls, Ma Perkinses, Bishop Mannings
and John L. Lewises they had only razzberries.
Long before naked women were the commonplaces
of every rotogravure supplement — indeed, long
before rotogravure supplements were invented —

large drawings of ladies in the altogether, usually in the then fashionable sepia chalk, decorated every newspaper art department in America. It was believed by young reporters that artists spent all their leisure in the company of such salacious creatures, and had their confidence. Even the most innocent young reporter, of course, was aware that they used no living models in their work, for everyone had noted how they systematically swiped from one another, so that a new aspect of the human frame, or of a dog's, or cat's, or elephant's frame, once it had appeared in a single newspaper in the United States, quickly reappeared in all the rest. But the artists fostered the impression that they did hand-painted oil-paintings on their days off, direct from nature unadorned. They let it be known that they were free spirits and much above the general, and in that character they sniffed at righteousness, whether on the high level of political and economic theory or the low one of ordinary police regulations.

I well recall the snobbish rage of a primeval comic-strip artist whom I once rebuked for using the office photographic equipment to make counterfeit five-dollar bills. It was on a Sunday morning, and I had dropped into the office for some reason forgotten. Hearing me shuffling around, he bounced out of the darkroom with a magnificent photograph of a fiver, cut precisely to scale, and invited me to admire it. I knew it would be useless to argue with him, but I was hardly prepared for his screams of choler when I grabbed the phoney, tore it up, and made off to the darkroom to smash the plate. He apparently regarded my action, not only as a personal insult, but also as an *attentat* against human enlightenment. If the word *bourgeois* had been in circulation at the time he would have flung it at me. As it was, he confined himself to likening my antipathy to counterfeit money to Lynn Meekins's Methodist aversion to drunkards, and laughed derisively at all the laws on the statute-books, from those against adultery to those prohibiting setting fire to zoos. I fired him on the spot, but took him back the next day, for good comic-strip artists were even more rare in that age than they are today.

Another that I fired — for what reason I forget — refused to come back when I sent for him, and I found on inquiry that he had got a job making side-show fronts for a one-ring circus. He produced such alarming bearded ladies, two-headed boys and wild men of Borneo that the circus went through the Valley of Virginia like wildfire, and in a little while he had orders from four or five of its rivals. By the end of a year he was the principal producer of side-show fronts south of the Mason & Dixon Line, and had three or four other artists working for him. Also, he had a new girl, and she appeared in public in clothes of very advanced cut, and presently took to drink. Undaunted, he put in another, and when she ran away with a minstrel-show press-agent, followed with a third, a fourth, and so on. Finally, one of them opened on him with a revolver, and he departed for Scranton, Pa. When he edged back to Baltimore a month or two later, glancing over his shoulder at every step, his business had been seized by his assistants, and the last I heard of him he was working for a third-rate instalment house, making improbable line drawings of parlor lamps, overstuffed sofas, washing-machines, and so on. Many other artists of that time went the same sad route. Starting out in life as painters of voluptuous nudes in the manner of Bouguereau, they finished as cogs in the mass production of line-cuts of ladies' hosiery.

In the heyday of this fellow I had a visit one day from a sacerdotal acquaintance — a Baptist clergyman who pastored a church down in the tide-water Carolinas. His customers, he told me, had lately made a great deal of money growing peanuts, and a new brick church was approaching completion in his parish. In this church was a large concrete baptismal tank — the largest south of Cape Hatteras — and it was fitted with all the latest gadgets, including a boiler downstairs to warm the water in cold weather. What it still lacked, said the pastor, was a suitable fancy background, and he had come to see me for advice and help on that point. Would it be possible to have a scene painted showing some of the principal events

of sacred history? If so, who would be a good man
to paint it? I thought at once of my side-show-
front friend, and in a little while I found him in a
barrel-house, and persuaded him to see the pastor.

The result was probably the most splendiferous
work of ecclesiastical art since the days of Michel-
angelo. On a canvas fifteen feet high and nearly
forty feet long the artist shot the whole works,
from the Creation as described in Genesis I to the
revolting events set forth in Revelation XIII.
Noah was there with his ark, and so was Solomon
in all his glory. No less than ten New Testament
miracles were depicted in detail, with the one at
Cana given the natural place of honor, and there
were at least a dozen battles of one sort or another,
including two between David and Goliath. The
Tower of Babel was made so high that it bled out
of the top of the painting, and there were three
separate views of Jerusalem. The sky showed a
dozen rainbows, and as many flashes of lightning,
and from a very red Red Sea in the foreground was
thrust the maw of Jonah's whale, with Jonah himself shinning out of it to join Moses and the children of Israel on the beach. This masterpiece was
completed in ten days, and brought $200 cash —
the price of ten side-show fronts. When it was
hung in the new Baptist church, it wrecked all the
other evangelical filling-stations of the lower Atlantic littoral, and people came from as far away
as Cleveland, Tenn., and Gainesville, Va., to wash

out their sins in the tank, and admire the art. The
artist himself was invited to submit to the process,
but replied stiffly that he was forbidden in conscience, for he professed to be an infidel.

The cops of those days, in so far as they were
aware of artists at all, accepted them at their own
valuation, and thus regarded them with suspicion.
If they were not actually on the level of water-front
crimps, dope-pedlars and piano-players in houses
of shame, they at least belonged somewhere south
of sporty doctors, professional bondsmen and
handbooks. This attitude once cost an artist of my
acquaintance his liberty for three weeks, though
he was innocent of any misdemeanor. On a cold
Winter night he and his girl lifted four or five ash-
boxes, made a roaring wood-fire in the fireplace of
his fourth-floor studio, and settled down to listen
to a phonograph, then a novelty in the world. The
glare of the blaze, shining red through the cob-
webbed windows, led a rookie cop to assume that
the house was afire, and he turned in an alarm.
When the firemen came roaring up, only to discover that the fire was in a fireplace, the poor cop
sought to cover his chagrin by collaring the artist,
and charging him with contributing to the delin-
quency of a minor. There was, of course, no truth
in this, for the lady was nearly forty years old and
had served at least two terms in a reformatory for
soliciting on the street, but the lieutenant at the
station-house, on learning that the culprit was an

artist, ordered him locked up for investigation, and he had been in the cooler three weeks before his girl managed to round up a committee of social-minded saloonkeepers to demand his release. The cops finally let him go with a warning, and for the rest of that Winter no artist in Baltimore dared to make a fire.

But it was not only artists themselves who suffered from the harsh uncharitableness of the world; they also conveyed something of their Poësque ill fortune to all their more intimate associates. I never knew an artist's girl, however beautiful, to marry anyone above a jail warden or a third-string jockey, and most of the early photo-engravers came to bad ends, often by suicide. The engravers used various violent poisons in their work, including cyanide of potassium. It was their belief that a dose of cyanide killed instantly and was thus painless, but every time one of them rounded out a big drunk by trying it he passed away in a tumultuous fit, and made a great deal of noise. The survivors, however, no more learned by experience than any other class of men, and cyanide remained their remedy of choice for the sorrows of this world. They had in their craft a sub-craft of so-called routers, whose job it was to deepen the spaces between the lines in line-cuts. This was done with a power-driven drill that bounced like a jumping-jack and was excessively inaccurate. If the cut was a portrait the router nearly always succeeded in routing out the eyes. Failing that, he commonly fetched one of his own fingers. Many's the time I have seen a routing machine clogged to a standstill by a mixture of zinc eyes and human tissue, with the router jumping around it with his hand under his arm, yelling for a doctor or a priest.

In those days halftones were not much used in newspapers, for it was only a few years since Stephen H. Horgan, of the New York *Tribune*, had discovered that they could be stereotyped. Most provincial stereotypers still made a mess of the job, so line-cuts were preferred, and relatively more artists were employed than today. Nevertheless, photographs were needed, if only to be copied in line, and every paper of any pretensions had at least one photographer. The first I recall on the *Herald* was a high-toned German of the name of Julius Seelander, who had served his apprenticeship in his native land. He wore a beard trimmed to display the large stickpin that glowed from his Ascot necktie: it was, in fact, *two* pins, with a filigree silver chain connecting them. Julius was an excellent technician, but had a habit of aesthetic abstraction in emergencies. Once, in bitter Winter weather, I took him along when I was assigned to go down the Chesapeake on an ice-boat, to cover the succoring of a fishing village that had been frozen in for weeks. We got to the place after a bumpy struggle through the ice, and Julius took a dozen swell pictures of the provisions going ashore and the starving oystermen fighting for them on the wharf. But when we got back to the office, and I was in the midst of my story, he came slinking out of his darkroom to confess that he had made all of the photographs on one plate. He said he was throwing up his job, and asked me to break the news to Max Ways: he was afraid that if he did so himself Max would stab him with a copy hook or throw him out of the window. But when I told Max he was very little perturbed, for he believed that all photographers, like all artists, were as grossly unreliable and deceptive as so many loaded dice, and it always surprised him when one of them carried out an assignment as ordered. The next day Julius was back in his darkroom, and so far as I know, nothing more was ever said about the matter.

But the most unfortunate camp-follower of art that I ever knew was not a photographer, nor even a photo-engraver, but a saloonkeeper named Kuno Something-or-other, who had a great many artists among his customers. When, in 1900, he opened a new saloon, they waited on him in a body, and offered to decorate its bare walls without a cent of cost to him, save only, of course, for their meals while they were at work, and a few drinks to stoke their aesthetic fires. Kuno, who loved everything artistic, jumped at the chance, and in a few days the first two of what was to be a long series of predacious frauds moved in on him. The pair daubed away for four or five hours a day, and it seemed to him, in the beginning, to be an excellent trade, for they not only got nothing for their services, but attracted a number of connoisseurs who watched them while they worked, and were good for an occasional flutter at the bar. But at the end of a couple of weeks, casting up accounts with his bartender, Kuno found that he was really breaking less than even, for while the credit side showed eight or ten square feet of wall embellished with beautiful girls in transparent underwear, the debit side ran to nearly 100 meals and more than 500 beers, all consumed by the artists.

Worse, the members of the succeeding teams were even hungrier and thirstier than the first pair, and by the time a fourth of one wall of the saloon was finished Kuno was in the red for more than 500 meals and nearly 7000 beers, not to mention innumerable whiskeys, absinthes and shots of bitters, and a couple of barrels of paint. The easy way out would have been to throw the artists into the street, but he respected the fine arts too much for that. Instead, he spent his days watching the Work in Progress and his nights trying to figure out how much he would be set back by the time it was finished. In the end these exercises unbalanced his mind, and he prepared to destroy himself, leaving his saloon half done, like a woman with one cheek made up and the other washed.

His exitus set an all-time high for technic, for he came from Frankfurt-an-der-Oder, and was a

Prussian for thoroughness. Going down to the
Long Bridge which spanned the Patapsco below
Baltimore, he climbed on the rail, fastened a long
rope to it, looped the other end around his neck,
swallowed a dose of arsenic, shot himself through
the head, and then leaped or fell into the river.
The old-time cops of Baltimore still astound rookies
with his saga. He remains the most protean performer they have ever had the pleasure of handling
post-mortem.

XI

THE DAYS OF THE

GIANTS

Not infrequently I am asked by young college folk, sometimes male and sometimes female, whether there has been any significant change, in my time, in the bacchanalian virtuosity of the American people. They always expect me, of course, to say that boozing is now at an all-time high, for they are a proud generation, and have been brought up to believe that Prohibition brought in refinements unparalleled on earth since the fall of Babylon. But when I speak for that thesis it is only to please them, for I know very well that the facts run the other way. My actual belief is that Americans reached the peak of their alcoholic puissance in the closing years of the last century. Along about 1903 there was a sudden and marked letting up — partly due, I suppose, to the accelerating pace and hazard of life in a civilization growing more and more mechanized, but also partly to be blamed on the lugubrious warnings of the medical men, who were then first learning how to reinforce their hocus-pocus with the alarms of the uplift.

In my early days as a reporter they had no more sense of civic responsibility than so many stockbrokers or policemen. A doctor of any standing not only had nothing to say against the use of stimulants; he was himself, nine times out of ten, a steady patron of them, and argued openly that they sustained him in his arduous and irregular life. Dr. Z. K. Wiley, our family practitioner, always took a snifter with my father when he dropped in to dose my brother Charlie and me with castor oil, and whenever, by some unusual accident of his heavy practise, he had any free time afterward, he and my father gave it over to quiet wrestling with the decanters. His favorite prescription for a cold was rock-and-rye, and he believed and taught that a shot of Maryland whiskey was the best preventive of pneumonia in the R months. If you object here that Dr. Wiley was a Southerner, then I answer at once that Dr. Oliver Wendell Holmes was a Yankee of the Yankees, and yet held exactly the same views. Every schoolboy, I suppose, has heard by this time of Dr. Holmes's famous address before the Massachusetts Medical

Society on May 30, 1860, in which he argued that "if the whole materia medica, as now used, could be sunk to the bottom of the sea, it would be all the better for mankind — and all the worse for the fishes"; but what the pedagogues always fail to tell their poor dupes is that he made a categorical exception of wine, which he ranked with opium, quinine, anesthetics and mercury among the sovereign and invaluable boons to humanity.

I was thus greatly surprised when I first heard a medical man talk to the contrary. This was in the Winter of 1899–1900, and the place was a saloon near a messy downtown fire. I was helping my betters to cover the fire, and followed them into the saloon for a prophylactic drink. The doctor, who was a fire department surgeon, thereupon made a speech arguing that alcohol was not a stimulant but a depressant, and advising us to keep off it until the fire was out and we were relaxing in preparation for bed. "You think it warms you," he said, sipping a hot milk, "but it really cools you, and you are seventeen point eight per cent. more likely to catch pneumonia at the present minute than you were when you came into this doggery." This heresy naturally outraged the older reporters, and they became so prejudiced against the doctor that they induced the Fire Board, shortly afterward, to can him — as I recall it, by reporting that he was always drunk on duty. But his words made a deep impression on my innocence, and continue to lurk in my mind to this day. In consequence, I am what may be called a somewhat cagey drinker. That is to say, I never touch the stuff by daylight if I can help it, and I employ it of an evening, not to hooch up my faculties, but to let them down after work. Not in years have I ever written anything with so much as a glass of beer in my system. My compositions, I gather, sometimes seem boozy to the nobility and gentry, but they are actually done as soberly as those of William Dean Howells.

But this craven policy is not general among the literati, nor was it to be noted among the journalists of my apprentice days. Between 1899 and 1904 there was only one reporter south of the Mason & Dixon Line who did not drink at all, and he was considered insane. In New York, so far as I could make out, there was not even one. On my first Christmas Eve on the *Herald* but two sober persons were to be found in the office — one of them a Seventh Day Adventist office-boy in the editorial rooms, and the other a superannuated stereotyper who sold lunches to the printers in the composing-room. There was a printer on the payroll who was reputed to be a teetotaler — indeed his singularity gave him the nickname of the Moral Element — , but Christmas Eve happened to be his night off. All the rest were full of what they called hand-set whiskey. This powerful drug was sold in a saloon next door to the *Herald* office, and was reputed to be made in the cellar by the proprietor in person — of wood alcohol, snuff, tabasco sauce, and coffin varnish. The printers liked it, and got down a great many shots of it. On the Christmas Eve I speak of its effects were such that more than half the linotype machines in the composing-room broke down, and one of the apprentices ran his shirt-tail through the proof-press. Down in the press-room four or five pressmen got hurt, and the city edition was nearly an hour late.

Nobody cared, for the head of the whole establishment, the revered managing editor, Colonel Cunningham, was locked up in his office with a case of Bourbon. At irregular intervals he would throw a wad of copy-paper over the partition which separated him from the editorial writers, and when this wad was smoothed out it always turned out to be part of an interminable editorial against General Felix Agnus, editor of the *American.* The General was a hero of the Civil War, with so much lead in his system that he was said to rattle as he walked, but Colonel Cunningham always hooted at his war record, and was fond of alleging — without any ground whatsoever — that he had come to America from his native France in the pussy-like character of a barber. The editorial that he was writing that Christmas Eve was headed, in fact, " The Barber of Seville." It never got into the paper, for it was running beyond three columns by press-time, and the night editor, Isidor Goodman, killed it for fear that its point was still to come. When the Colonel inquired about it two or three days afterward he was told that a truck had upset in the composing-room, and pied it.

The hero of the *Herald* composing-room in those days was a fat printer named Bill, who was reputed to be the champion beer-drinker of the Western Hemisphere. Bill was a first-rate linotype operator, and never resorted to his avocation in working-hours, but the instant his time was up he would hustle on his coat and go to a beer-house in the neighborhood, and there give what he called a setting. He made no charge for admission, but the spectators, of course, were supposed to pay for the beer. One night in 1902 I saw him get down thirty-two bottles in a row. Perhaps, in your wanderings, you have seen the same — but have you ever heard of a champion who could do it *without once retiring from his place at the bar?* Well, that is what Bill did, and on another occasion, when I was not present, he reached forty. Physiologists tell me that these prodigies must have been optical delusions, for there is not room enough in the coils and recesses of man for so much liquid, but I can only reply *Pfui* to that, for a record is a record. Bill avoided the door marked " Gents " as diligently as if he had been a débutante of the era, or the sign on it had been " For Ladies Only." He would have been humiliated beyond endurance if anyone had ever seen him slink through it.

In the year 1904, when the *Herald* office was destroyed in the great Baltimore fire, and we had to print the paper, for five weeks, in Philadelphia, I was told off to find accommodation for the printers. I found it in one of those old-fashioned $1-a-day hotels that were all bar on the first floor. The proprietor, a German with goat whiskers, was somewhat reluctant to come to terms, for he had heard that printers were wild fellows who might be expected to break up his furniture and work their wicked will upon his chambermaids, but when I told him that a beer-champion was among them he showed a more friendly interest, and when I began to brag about Bill's extraordinary talents his doubts disappeared and he proposed amiably that some Philadelphia foam-jumpers be invited in to make it a race. The first heat was run the very next night, and Bill won hands down. In fact, he won so easily that he offered grandly to go until he had drunk *twice* as much as the next best entry. We restrained him and got him to bed, for there had been some ominous whispering among the other starters, and it was plain that they were planning to call in help. The next night it appeared in the shape of a tall, knotty man from Allentown, Pa., who was introduced as the champion of the Lehigh Valley. He claimed to be not only a beer-drinker of high gifts, but also a member of the Bach Choir at Bethlehem; and when he got down his first dozen mugs — the boys were drinking from the wood — he cut

loose with an exultant yodel that he said was one
of Bach's forgotten minor works. But he might
very well have saved his wind, for Bill soon had
him, and at the end of the setting he was four or
five mugs behind, and in a state resembling suffocation. The next afternoon I saw his disconsolate
fans taking him home, a sadder and much less melo-
dious man.

On the first two nights there had been only slim
galleries, but on the third the bar was jammed, and
anyone could see that something desperate was
afoot. It turned out to be the introduction of two
super-champions, the one a short, saturnine Welshman from Wilkes-Barré, and the other a hearty
blond young fellow from one of the Philadelphia
suburbs, who said that he was half German and
half Irish. The Welshman was introduced as the
man who had twice drunk Otto the Brewery Horse
under the table, and we were supposed to know who
Otto was, though we didn't. The mongrel had a
committee with him, and the chairman thereof offered to lay $25 on him at even money. The print-
ers in Bill's corner made up the money at once, and
their stake had grown to $50 in forty minutes by
the clock, for the hybrid took only that long to
blow up. The Welshman lasted much better, and
there were some uneasy moments when he seemed
destined to make history again by adding Bill to
Otto, but in the end he succumbed so suddenly that
it seemed like a bang, and his friends laid him out

on the floor and began fanning him with bar-towels.

Bill was very cocky after that, and talked gran-diosely of taking on two champions at a time, in marathon series. There were no takers for several nights, but after that they began to filter in from the remoter wilds of the Pennsylvania Dutch coun-try, and the whole *Herald* staff was kept busy guarding Bill by day, to make sure that he did not waste any of his libido for malt liquor in the after-noons. He knocked off twenty or thirty challengers during the ensuing weeks, including two more Welshmen from the hard-coal country, a Scots-man with an ear missing, and a bearded Dunkard from Lancaster county. They were mainly push-overs, but now and then there was a tough one. Bill did not let this heavy going interfere with the practise of his profession. He set type every night from 6 p.m. to midnight in the office of the *Evening Telegraph*, where we were printing the *Herald*, and never began his combats until 12.30. By two o'clock he was commonly in bed, with another wreath of laurels hanging on the gas-jet.

To ease your suspense I'll tell you at once that he was never beaten. Germans, Irishmen, Welsh-men and Scotsmen went down before him like so many Sunday-school superintendents, and he bowled over everyday Americans with such facil-ity that only two of them ever lasted more than half an hour. But I should add in candor that he

was out of service during the last week of our stay
in Philadelphia. What fetched him is still a subject of debate among the pathologists at the Johns
Hopkins Medical School, to whom the facts were
presented officially on our return to Baltimore.
The only visible symptom was a complete loss of
speech. Bill showed up one night talking hoarsely,
the next night he could manage only whispers, and
the third night he was as mute as a shad-fish.
There was absolutely no other sign of distress. He
was all for going on with his derisive harrying of
the Pennsylvania lushers, but a young doctor who
hung about the saloon and served as surgeon at the
bouts forbade it on unstated medical grounds. The
Johns Hopkins experts in morbid anatomy have
never been able to agree about the case. Some
argue that Bill's potations must have dissolved the
gummy coating of his pharyngeal plexus, and thus
paralyzed his vocal cords; the rest laugh at this as
nonsense savoring of quackery, and lay the whole
thing to an intercurrent laryngitis, induced by insufficient bedclothes on very cold nights. I suppose
that no one will ever know the truth. Bill recovered
his voice in a couple of months, and soon afterward
left Baltimore. Of the prodigies, if any, that
marked his later career I can't tell you.

He was but one of a notable series of giants who
flourished in Baltimore at the turn of the century,
bringing the city a friendly publicity and causing
the theory to get about that life there must be de-

lightful. They appeared in all the ranks of society. The Maryland Club had its champions, and the cops had theirs. Some were drinkers pure and simple; others specialized in eating. One of the latter was an old man of easy means who lived at the Rennert Hotel, then the undisputed capital of gastronomy in the terrapin and oyster country. But for some reason that I can't tell you he never did his eating there; instead, he always took dinner at Tommy McPherson's eating-house, six or eight blocks away. He would leave the hotel every evening at seven o'clock, elegantly arrayed in a long-tailed black coat and a white waistcoat, and carrying a gold-headed cane, and would walk the whole way. Tommy's place was arranged in two layers, with tables for men only alongside the bar downstairs, and a series of small rooms upstairs to which ladies might be invited. The cops, goaded by vice crusaders, had forced him to take the doors off these rooms, but he had substituted heavy portières, and his colored waiters were instructed to make a noise as they shuffled down the hall, and to enter every room backward. The old fellow I speak of, though there were tales about his wild youth, had by now got beyond thought of sin, and all his eating was done downstairs. It consisted of the same dishes precisely every night of the week, year in and year out. First he would throw in three straight whiskeys, and then he would sit down to *two* double porterhouse steaks, with *two* large plates of peas, *two* of French fried potatoes, *two* of cole-slaw, and a mountain of rye-bread. This vast meal he would eat to the last speck, and not infrequently he called for more potatoes or bread. He washed it down with two quarts of Burgundy, and at its end threw in three more straight whiskeys. Then he would light a cigar, and amble back to the Rennert, to spend the rest of the evening conversing with the politicoes who made their headquarters in its lobby.

One day a report reached the *Herald* office that he was beginning to break up, and Max Ways sent me to take a look. He had, by then, been on his diet for no less than twelve years. When I opened the subject delicately he hooted at the notion that he was not up to par. He was, he told me, in magnificent health, and expected to live at least twenty years longer. His excellent condition, he went on to say, was due wholly to his lifelong abstemiousness. He ate only a sparing breakfast, and no lunch at all, and he had not been drunk for fifteen years — that is, in the sense of losing all control of himself. He told me that people who ate pork dug their graves with their teeth, and praised the Jews for avoiding it. He also said that he regarded all sea-food as poisonous, on the ground that it contained too much phosphorus, and that fowl was almost as bad. There was, in his view, only one perfectly safe and wholesome victual, and that was beef. It had everything. It was nourishing, palat-

able and salubrious. The last bite tasted as good
as the first. Even the bones had a pleasant flavor.
He ate peas and potatoes with it, he said, mainly
to give it some company: if he were ever cast on a
desert island he could do without them. The cole-
slaw went along as a sort of gesture of politeness
to the grass that had produced the beef, and he ate
rye-bread instead of wheat because rye was the
bone and sinew of Maryland whiskey, the most
healthful appetizer yet discovered by man. He
would not affront me by presuming to discuss the
virtues of Burgundy: they were mentioned in the
Bible, and all humanity knew them.

The old boy never made his twenty years, but
neither did he ever change his regimen. As the uplift gradually penetrated medicine various doctors
of his acquaintance began to warn him that he was
headed for a bad end, but he laughed at them in
his quiet way, and went on going to Tommy's place
every night, and devouring his two double porter-
houses. What took him off at last was not his eating, but a trifling accident. He was knocked down
by a bicycle in front of the Rennert, developed
pneumonia, and was dead in three days. The
resurrection men at both the Johns Hopkins and
the University of Maryland tried to get his body
for autopsy, and were all set to dig out of it a whole
series of pathological monstrosities of a moral tendency, but his lawyer forbade any knifeplay until
his only heir, a niece, could be consulted, and when

she roared in from Eufaula, Ala., it turned out
that she was a Christian Scientist, with a hate
against anatomy. So he was buried without yielding any lessons for science. If he had any real
rival, in those declining years of Baltimore gastronomy, it must have been John Wilson, a cop:
I have always regretted that they were never
brought together in a match. Once, at a cop party,
I saw John eat thirty fried hard crabs at a sitting
— no mean feat, I assure you, for though the claws
are pulled off a crab before it is fried, all the body-
meat remains. More, he not only ate the crabs, but
sucked the shells. On another occasion, on a bet,
he ate a ham and a cabbage in half an hour by the
clock, but I was not present at that performance.
When, a little later, he dropped dead in the old
Central station-house, the police surgeons laid it
to a pulmonary embolus, then a recent novelty in
pathology.

XII

THE

JUDICIAL ARM

My recollection of judges and my veneration for them go back a long way before my newspaper days, for I was a boy not more than eight or nine years old when my father began taking me on his tours of the more high-toned Washington saloons, and pointing out for my edification the eminent men who infested them. Not a few of those dignitaries were ornaments of the Federal judiciary, and among them were some whose names were almost household words in the Republic. But it was not their public fame that most impressed me; it was the lordly and elegant way in which they did their boozing. Before I really knew what a Congressman was I was aware that Congressmen were bad actors in barrooms, and often had to be thrown out, and years before I had heard that the United States Senate sat in trials of impeachment and formerly had a say in international treaties I had seen a Senator stricken by the first acrobatic symptoms of delirium tremens. But though I search my memory diligently, and it is especially tenacious in sociological matters, I can't recall a single judge who ever showed any sign of yielding to the influence. They all drank freely, and with a majestic spaciousness of style, but they carried their liquor like gentlemen.

Boy-like, I must have assumed that this gift for the bottle ran with their high station, and was, in fact, a part of their professional equipment, for I remember being greatly astonished years later, when I first encountered, as a young reporter, a judge definitely in his cups. There was nothing to the story save the bald fact that the poor old man, facing a hard calendar in equity on a morning when he was nursing a hangover from a Bar Association banquet, had thrown in one too many quick ones, and so got himself plastered. When he fell sound asleep in his pulpit, with his feet on the bench, there was a considerable pother, and by the time I wandered upon the scene his bailiffs had evacuated him to his chambers and doused him with ice-water, and he was rapidly resuming rationality, as his loud swearing indicated. Being still innocent, I reported the facts truthfully to Max Ways, and was somewhat puzzled when he ordered me to write a brief piece saying that His Honor had been floored at the post of duty by stomach ulcers, but was happily out of danger. Later on, as my journalistic experience widened, I saw many judges in a more or less rocky state, though I should add at once that I never saw another in that condition on the actual bench or within its purlieus, and that most of those I encountered were very far from their own courts. Indeed, I gradually picked up the impression that judges, like police captains, never really let themselves go until they were away from home. In those days all the police captains of the Eastern seaboard, whenever they felt that they couldn't stand the horrors of their office another minute, went to Atlantic City, and there soused and bellowed incognito, without either public scandal or danger to their jobs. Sometimes as many as a dozen gathered in one saloon — two or three from New York, a couple each from Philadelphia, Baltimore and Washington, and maybe the rest from points as far west as Pittsburgh. In the same way judges commonly sought a hide-away when the impulse to cut loose was on them; in their own archdioceses they kept their thirsts in hand, and so avoided the prying eyes of the vulgar.

At the time I began to find my way about as a reporter there was a rich old fellow in Baltimore who gave a big stag dinner every year at the Maryland Club. He was himself of no prominence, and his dinner had no public significance: it was simply that he loved good eating and enlightened boozing himself, and delighted in getting a group of men of the same mind about him. He had begun long before with a relatively small party, but every year the grateful patients suggested that it would be nice to include this or that recruit, and in the era I speak of the feast had grown to be very large and surpassingly elaborate, with seventy or eighty head of guests at the long table, as many colored waiters toting in the oysters, wild duck and terrapin, a large staff of sommeliers at the wine-buckets, and a battery of bartenders out in the hall. One year a judge was among the delegation of stockbrokers, bank presidents, wine-agents, Tammany leaders and other dignitaries who came down from New York, and the next year he brought another, and the year following there were three, and then six, and so on. They greatly enjoyed the entertainment, and no wonder, for it was in the best Maryland Club manner; and the host, on his side, appreciated having so many men of mark at his board. But in the course of time it began to be hard on the families of some of the judges, and almost as hard on the cops and newspaper reporters of Baltimore.

For every time there was a dinner it launched a drunk in the grand manner, and every time there was such a drunk the job of rounding up the judiciary took two or three days, and was full of embarrassments and alarms. Many of the other guests, of course, also succumbed to the grape, but no one ever seemed to care what had become of them. A Tammany leader could disappear for two days, and cause no remark; even a bank president would not be posted at Lloyd's until the third day. But judges, it appeared, were missed very quickly, if not by their catchpolls then certainly by their wives and daughters, and by the late afternoon of the day after the dinner inquiries about this or that one would begin to come in from the North. Not infrequently the inquiry would be lodged in person by a frantic daughter, and when she was put off by the cops with weasel words she would tour the newspaper offices, declaring hysterically that her pa must have been murdered, and demanding the immediate production of his carcass.

The cops were indifferent for a plain reason: they always knew where the missing judges were. So, in fact, did everybody know, but it was not etiquette to say so. For aside from a few very ancient men who had gone direct from the dinner to the nervous diseases ward of the Johns Hopkins Hospital, and were there undergoing the ammonia cure, all the recreant Pontius Pilates were safely housed in the stews of Baltimore, which were then surpassed in luxury and polish only by the stews of St. Louis. Every such establishment had appropriate accommodations for just such clients. They would be lodged in comfortable rooms, watched over by trustworthy bouncers, entertained with music, dancing and easy female conversation, and supplied with booze until they seemed about to give out, whereupon they would be put on strict rations of milk and soda-water and so prepared for restoration to the world. All the chatêlaines of the Baltimore houses of sin were familiar with that kind of trade, and knew precisely how to handle it, for they got a great deal of it, year in and year out, from Washington. Having handled maniacal Senators and Ambassadors, not to mention even higher dignitaries, they were not daunted by a sudden rush of harmless judges.

Unhappily, it was hard to convince the daughters of the missing jurists that they were comfortable and happy, and under no hazards to either their lives or their morals. Every such inquirer refused violently to be placated with generalizations: she demanded to be taken to her father instantly, and allowed to convoy him home. Inasmuch as no one dared to tell her where he was, it became the custom to say that he had gone down to a ducking club on the Eastern Shore of Maryland, and was there engaged in shooting mallards and canvasbacks. But there were always daughters who declared that their fathers were not marksmen, and in fact had a fear of guns, and sometimes it took a good deal of blarney to convince them that duck-shooting could be learned in half an hour, and was done with air-rifles or sling-shots.

Even those who swallowed the lie often made trouble, for they usually proposed to proceed to the duck country at once, and I recall one who spent two days and nights roving the Eastern Shore, seeking some trace of a tall old man wearing a heavy white moustache, weighing 220 pounds, and dressed in a broadcloth cutaway and striped pants. It would have done no good to tell this poor lady that her father was still wearing the evening clothes that he had put on for the dinner. All the visitors, in fact, continued in their tails until the time came to wash them up and start them home. The champion in my day went on thus for four days and nights, and when the whistle was blown on him at last his judicial collar, white lawn tie and boiled shirt were in a truly scandalous state. Within the month following his return to duty, so I was told afterward, he sentenced five men to death.

How the old boys accounted for their disappearance to their daughters, once they had got back to their hotels and changed clothes for the journey home, I do not know, and never inquired. I suppose that a daughter is bound in law to believe anything her father tells her, especially if he be a judge, and I assume that judges, having been lawyers, have good imaginations and ready tongues. All I can tell you is that this annual man-hunt was a headache to the city editors of Baltimore, and to their faithful reporters. We had to keep watch on the whole gang for two or three days and nights, ever full of a pardonable hope that this one or that one would fall out of a window, brain a piano-player, drop dead of *mania à potu*, or otherwise qualify for our professional attentions. It would never do to be beaten on such a story — if such a story ever bobbed up. But it never did. The judges all got home safely, and whenever it turned out that one of them had left his watch behind, or his wallet, or his plug hat, the cops always recovered it promptly, and turned it over to the host, who saw that it was restored to its owner.

There was in those days a standard Maryland dinner for all festive occasions, and it was eaten five hundred times a year in the more polished hotels and clubs of Baltimore. It had the strange peculiarity of being wholly devoid of vegetables: every item on the bill save the salad was protein, and even the salad had slices of ham in it. It began with Chesapeake Bay oysters, proceeded to Chesapeake Bay terrapin, went on to Chesapeake Bay wild ducks, and then petered out in lettuce salad with Smithfield ham, and harlequin ice-cream. Sometimes a thin soup was served between the oysters and the terrapin, but often not. The oysters were not the rachitic dwarfs now seen on dinner tables, but fat, yellow, eunuchoid monsters at least six inches long; indeed, they were frequently nearer ten than six. A stranger to the Maryland cuisine, confronting such an oyster for the first time, usually got into a panic, but his host always bucked him up to trying it on his esophagus, and when he did so it commonly went down without choking him, for an oyster is a very pliant and yielding animal, and is also well lubricated. To cut up one would be regarded, in Maryland, as an indecency to be matched only by frying soft crabs in batter or putting cream into terrapin stew. The last two crimes against humanity obtain in New York, Philadelphia and Washington, but not in Baltimore. Soft crabs are always fried (or broiled) there in the altogether, with maybe a small jockstrap of bacon added, and nothing goes with terrapin save butter, seasoning and a jigger or two of sherry. Today a Marylander will give humble thanks to God for any kind of wild duck he can shoot, trap, beg, bootleg or steal, but in the Golden Age he offered his guests only the breasts of canvasbacks. Along with the orthodox dinner that I have outlined went an equally rigid programme of drinks. If cocktails were served before going to the table they had to be Manhattans, for no Baltimorean of condition ever drank gin: it was for blackamoors only, with a humane reservation in favor of white ladies suffering from female weakness. With the terrapin came sherry, or maybe Madeira, and with the duck, champagne, or maybe Burgundy. The rest of the dinner was washed down with champagne only, and the more of it the better.

This bill-of-fare, with all the drinks save the

cocktails included, cost $10 a plate in any good
Baltimore hotel. In that age of low living costs it
was a high price, and the persons who paid it tried
to get the worth of their money by guzzling all the
champagne they could hold. As a young reporter
I covered many such dinners, and saw some drinking bouts of very high amperage. The annual
banquet of the Merchants and Manufacturers Association, then the chief organization of the local
Babbitti, always ended in one of them. The chief
speaker was usually either the Governor of some
Southern state or a United States Senator, but it
was seldom that his remarks were heard by anyone
save the reporters and a few old Presbyterian
misers, for all the rest of the guests were far gone
by the time he got up, and not infrequently he was
pretty well smeared himself. As I have noted, it
was nothing to me to see a Senator in his cups, but
it always shocked the Presbyterians, and after
every dinner they proposed that the next one be
dry. This proposal, when it got into the newspapers, set off a debate that went on for weeks and
invariably ended in one way, with Colonel Cunningham and General Agnus joined in brotherly
amity on the triumphant wet side. No M. & M.
party was ever even ostensibly dry until the Prohibition murrain came down upon the country. The
classical Maryland dinner was one of that great
curse's first victims, and has never been revived,
for when Prohibition went out at last new game

laws came in, and it would be impossible today to assemble enough canvasback ducks to feed 500 men, or even fifty. In the midst of the thirteen doleful years the M. & M. itself gave up the ghost, and was absorbed by a new organization which devotes itself mainly to shipping and manufacturing statistics, and is not interested in the good living which once made Baltimore the envy of every other American city save New Orleans.

XIII

RECOLLECTIONS OF

NOTABLE COPS

Some time ago I read in a New York paper that fifty or sixty college graduates had been appointed to the metropolitan police force, and were being well spoken of by their superiors. The news astonished me, for in my reportorial days there was simply no such thing in America as a book-learned cop, though I knew a good many who were very smart. The force was then recruited, not from the groves of Academe, but from the ranks of working-men. The best police captain I ever knew in Baltimore was a meat-cutter by trade, and had lost one of his thumbs by a slip of his cleaver, and the next best was a former bartender. All the mounted cops were ex-hostlers passing as ex-cavalrymen, and all the harbor police had come up through the tugboat and garbage-scow branches of the merchant marine. It took a young reporter a little while to learn how to read and interpret the reports that cops turned in, for they were couched in a special kind of English, with a spelling peculiar to itself. If a member of what was then called " the finest " had spelled *larceny* in any way save *larsensy,* or *arson* in any way save *arsony,* or *fracture* in any way save *fraxr,* there would have been a considerable lifting of eyebrows. I well recall the horror of the Baltimore cops when the first board to examine applicants for places on the force was set up. It was a harmless body headed by a political dentist, and the hardest question in its first examination paper was " What is the plural of *ox?,*" but all the cops in town predicted that it would quickly contaminate their craft with a great horde of what they called " professors," and reduce it to the level of letter-carrying or school-teaching.

But, as I have noted, their innocence of *literae humaniores* was not necessarily a sign of stupidity, and from some of them, in fact, I learned the valuable lesson that sharp wits can lurk in unpolished skulls. I knew cops who were matches for the most learned and unscrupulous lawyers at the Baltimore bar, and others who had made monkeys of the oldest and crabbedest judges on the bench, and were generally respected for it. Moreover, I knew cops who were really first-rate policemen, and loved their trade as tenderly as so many art artists or movie actors. They were badly paid, but they carried on their dismal work with unflagging diligence, and loved a long, hard chase almost as much as they loved a quick, brisk clubbing. Their one salient failing, taking them as a class, was their belief that any person who had been arrested, even on mere suspicion, was unquestionably and *ipso facto* guilty. But that theory, though it occasionally colored their testimony in a garish manner, was grounded, after all, on nothing worse than professional pride and *esprit de corps*, and I am certainly not one to hoot at it, for my own belief in the mission of journalism has no better support than the same partiality, and all the logic I am aware of stands against it.

In those days that pestilence of Service which torments the American people today was just getting under way, and many of the multifarious duties now carried out by social workers, statisticians, truant officers, visiting nurses, psychologists, and the vast rabble of inspectors, smellers, spies and bogus experts of a hundred different faculties either fell to the police or were not discharged at all. An ordinary flatfoot in a quiet residential section had his hands full. In a single day he might have to put out a couple of kitchen fires, arrange for the removal of a dead mule, guard a poor epileptic having a fit on the sidewalk, catch a runaway horse, settle a combat with table knives between husband and wife, shoot a cat for killing pigeons rescue a dog or a baby from a sewer, bawl out a white-wings for spilling garbage, keep order on the sidewalk at two or three funerals, and flog half a dozen bad boys for throwing horse-apples at a blind man. The cops downtown, especially along the wharves and in the red-light districts, had even more curious and complicated jobs, and some of them attained to a high degree of virtuosity.

As my memory gropes backward I think, for example, of a strange office that an old-time roundsman named Charlie had to undertake every Spring. It was to pick up enough skilled workmen to effect the annual re-decoration and refurbishing of the Baltimore City Jail. Along about May 1 the warden would telephone to police headquarters that he needed, say, ten head of painters, five plumbers, two blacksmiths, a tile-setter, a roofer, a bricklayer, a carpenter and a locksmith, and it was Charlie's duty to go out and find them. So far as I can recall, he never failed, and usually he produced two or three times as many craftsmen of each category as were needed, so that the warden had some chance to pick out good ones. His plan was simply to make a tour of the saloons and stews in the Marsh Market section of Baltimore, and look over the drunks in congress assembled. He had a trained eye, and could detect a plumber or a painter through two weeks' accumulation of beard and dirt. As he gathered in his candidates, he searched them on the spot, rejecting those who had no union cards, for he was a firm believer in organized labor. Those who passed were put into storage at a police-station, and there kept (less the unfortunates who developed delirium tremens and had to be handed over to the resurrection-men) until the whole convoy was ready. The next morning Gene Grannan, the police magistrate, gave them two weeks each for vagrancy, loitering, trespass, committing a nuisance, or some other plausible misdemeanor, the warden had his staff of master-workmen, and the jail presently bloomed out in all its vernal finery.

Some of these toilers returned year after year, and in the end Charlie recognized so many that he could accumulate the better part of his convoy in half an hour. Once, I remember, he was stumped by a call for two electricians. In those remote days there were fewer men of that craft in practise than today, and only one could be found. When the warden put on the heat Charlie sent him a trolley-car motorman who had run away from his wife and was trying to be shanghaied for the Chesapeake oyster-fleet. This poor man, being grateful for his security in jail, made such eager use of his meagre electrical knowledge that the warden decided to keep him, and even requested that his sentence be extended. Unhappily, Gene Grannan was a pretty good amateur lawyer, and knew that such an extension would be illegal. When the warden of the House of Correction, which was on a farm

twenty miles from Baltimore, heard how well this
system was working, he put in a requisition for six
experienced milkers and a choir-leader, for he had
a herd of cows and his colored prisoners loved to
sing spirituals. Charlie found the choir-leader in
no time, but he bucked at hunting for milkers, and
got rid of the nuisance by sending the warden a
squad of sailors who almost pulled the poor cows
to pieces.

Gene had been made a magistrate as one of the
first fruits of the rising reform movement in Baltimore, and was a man of the chastest integrity, but
he knew too much about reformers to admire them,
and lost no chance to afflict them. When, in 1900,
or thereabout, a gang of snoopers began to tour
the red-light districts, seeking to harass and alarm
the poor working women there denizened, he instructed the gals to empty slops on them, and acquitted all who were brought in for doing it, usually on the ground that the complaining witnesses
were disreputable persons, and could not be believed on oath. One day, sitting in his frowsy
courtroom, I saw him gloat in a positively indecent
manner when a Methodist clergyman was led out
from the cells by Mike Hogan, the turnkey. This
holy man, believing that the Jews, unless they con-
sented to be baptized, would all go to Hell, had
opened a mission in what was then still called the
Ghetto, and sought to save them. The adults, of
course, refused to have anything to do with him,

but he managed, after a while, to lure a number of *kosher* small boys into his den, chiefly by showing them magic-lantern pictures of the Buffalo Bill country and the Holy Land. When their fathers heard of this there was naturally an uproar, for it was a mortal sin in those days for an orthodox Jew to enter a *Goy Schul.* The ritual for delousing offenders was an arduous one, and cost both time and money. So the Jews came clamoring to Grannan, and he spent a couple of hours trying to figure out some charge to lay against the evangelist. Finally, he ordered him brought in, and entered him on the books for " annoying persons passing by and along a public highway, disorderly conduct, making loud and unseemly noises, and disturbing religious worship." He had to be acquitted, of course, but Gene scared him so badly with talk of the penitentiary that he shut down his mission forthwith, and left the Jews to their post-mortem sufferings.

As I have noted in Chapter II, Gene was a high favorite among us young reporters, for he was always good for copy, and did not hesitate to modify the course of justice in order to feed and edify us. One day an ancient German, obviously a highly respectable man, was brought in on the incredible charge of beating his wife. The testimony showed that they had been placidly married for more than 45 years, and seldom exchanged so much as a bitter word. But the night before, when the old man came home from the saloon where he played *Skat* every evening, the old woman accused him of having drunk more than his usual ration of eight beers, and in the course of the ensuing debate he gave her a gentle slap. Astounded, she let off an hysterical squawk, an officious neighbor rushed in, the cops came on his heels, and so the old man stood before the bar of justice, weeping copiously and with his wife weeping even more copiously beside him. Gene pondered the evidence with a frown on his face, and then announced his judgment. " The crime you are accused of committing," he said, " is a foul and desperate one, and the laws of all civilized countries prohibit it under heavy penalties. I could send you to prison for life, I could order you to the whipping-post [it still exists in Maryland, and for wife-beaters only], or I could sentence you to be hanged. [Here both parties screamed.] But inasmuch as this is your first offense I will be lenient. You will be taken hence to the House of Correction, and there confined for twenty years. In addition, you are fined $10,000." The old couple missed the fine, for at mention of the House of Correction both fainted. When the cops revived them, Gene told the prisoner that, on reflection, he had decided to strike out the sentence, and bade him go and sin no more. Husband and wife rushed out of the court-room hand in hand, followed by a cop with the umbrella and market-basket that the old woman had forgotten. A week or two later news came in that she was ordering the old man about in a highly

cavalier manner, and had cut down his evenings of
Skat to four a week.

The cops liked and admired Gene, and when he
was in good form he commonly had a gallery of
them in his courtroom, guffawing at his whimsies.
But despite his popularity among them he did not
pal with them, for he was basically a very dignified,
and even somewhat stiff fellow, and knew how to
call them down sharply when their testimony before him went too far beyond the bounds of the
probable. In those days, as in these, policemen led
a social life almost as inbred as that of the justices
of the Supreme Court of the United States, and
outsiders were seldom admitted to their parties.
But reporters were exceptions, and I attended a
number of cop soirées of great elegance, with the
tables piled mountain-high with all the delicacies
of the season, and a keg of beer every few feet. The
graft of these worthy men, at least in my time, was
a great deal less than reformers alleged and the envious common people believed. Most of them, in
my judgment, were very honest fellows, at least
within the bounds of reason. Those who patrolled
the fish-markets naturally had plenty of fish to
eat, and those who manned the police-boats in the
harbor took a certain toll from the pungy captains
who brought up Baltimore's supplies of water-
melons, cantaloupes, vegetables, crabs and oysters
from the Eastern Shore of Maryland: indeed, this
last impost amounted to a kind of *octroi*, and at

one time the harbor force accumulated so much provender that they had to seize an empty warehouse on the waterfront to store it. But the pungy captains gave up uncomplainingly, for the pelagic cops protected them against the thieves and highjackers who swarmed in the harbor, and also against the land police. I never heard of cops getting anything that the donor was not quite willing and even eager to give. Every Italian who ran a peanut stand knew that making them free of it was good institutional promotion and the girls in the red-light districts liked to crochet neckties, socks and pulse-warmers for them. It was not unheard of for a cop to get mashed on such a girl, rescue her from her life of shame, and set her up as a more or less honest woman. I knew of several cases in which holy matrimony followed. But the more ambitious girls, of course, looked higher, and some of them, in my time, made very good marriages. One actually married a banker, and another died only a few years ago as the faithful and much respected wife of a prominent physician. The cops always laughed when reformers alleged that the wages of sin were death — specifically, that women who sold their persons always ended in the gutter, full of dope and despair. They knew that the overwhelming majority ended at the altar of God, and that nearly all of them married better men than they could have had any chance of meeting and roping if they had kept their virtue.

One dismal New Year's day I saw a sergeant lose an excellent chance to pocket $138.66 in cash money: I remember it brilliantly because I lost the same chance at the same moment. There had been the usual epidemic of suicides in the waterfront flop-houses, for the dawn of a new year turns the thoughts of homeless men to peace beyond the dissecting-room, and I accompanied the sergeant and a coroner on a tour of the fatal scenes. One of the dead men was lying on the fifth floor of a decaying warehouse that had been turned into ten-cent sleeping quarters, and we climbed up the long stairs to inspect him. All the other bums had cleared out, and the hophead clerk did not offer to go with us. We found the deceased stretched out in a peaceful attitude, with the rope with which he had hanged himself still around his neck. He had been cut down, but then abandoned.

The sergeant loosed the rope, and began a search of the dead man's pockets, looking for means to identify him. He found nothing whatever of that sort, but from a pants pocket he drew out a fat wad of bills, and a hasty count showed that it contained $416. A situation worthy of Scribe, or even Victor Hugo! Evidently the poor fellow was one of the Russell Sages that are occasionally found among bums. His money, I suppose, had been diminishing, and he had bumped himself off in fear that it would soon be all gone. The sergeant looked at the coroner, the coroner looked at me, and I looked at the sergeant. Then the sergeant wrapped up the money in a piece of newspaper lying nearby, and handed it to the coroner. " It goes," he said sadly, " to the State of Maryland. The son-of-a-bitch died intestate, and with no heirs."

The next day I met the coroner, and found him in a low frame of mind. " It was a sin and a shame," he said, " to turn that money over to the State Treasury. What I could have done with $138.67! (I noticed he made a fair split, but collared one of the two odd cents.) Well, it's gone now — damn the luck! I never *did* trust that flat-foot."

XIV

A

GENIAL RESTAURANTEUR

I AM well aware that the word *restauranteur*, as it appears in the title of this chapter, contains an *n* that the French eschew; my plea in confession and avoidance must be that I am not writing French but American, and, specifically, the American in vogue on the newspapers of my native Baltimore in my salad days as a journalist. No reporter of that era ever thought of referring to a respectable saloonkeeper as a saloonkeeper: the term was reserved, at least in print, for such dubious characters as Bob Fosbender, whose place at Pine and Raborg streets was the very Capitol of the Western red-light district — and when I say Capitol I mean exactly that, for the representative assembly of the adjacent landladies, always called simply the Senate, met in his back room once a week. All saloonkeepers above Bob's social and moral level, with one exception, were restauranteurs, with the *n*, and all that were personally known to newspaper men, and held in reasonable esteem, rated the *genial* in front of *restauranteur*.

This large company included even Frank Junker, probably one of the least genial men, in actuality, that ever suffered from varicose veins, the occupational malady of all the old-timers of his profession. He was a stout, short, silent, suspicious German who was a Scotsman in all save the husk or rind, and he owned a modest but very profitable saloon opposite the Baltimore City Hall. Having learned by experience that municipal job-holders, as a class, were grasping and cantankerous men, he did not cater to them, but directed his lures (*a*) to the musicians, stagehands and ham actors of the old Holliday Street Theatre, which was half a block away, and (*b*) to journalists. Neither of these groups had any great amount of money, but they could be trusted to spend all they had, and, moreover, they spread their boozing over both day and night. Like any other downtown saloonkeeper Frank had plenty of business in daylight hours, but at night most of the streets near the City Hall were as dead as Herculaneum, and many of the genial restauranteurs in them actually closed at 9 p.m. But not this one, for he had learned that that was the hour when musicians and actors began to duck out for really earnest drinking, and he knew, too, that journalists hardly got under way until an hour or two later. Thus his place was crowded every night, and I have seen it so jammed at midnight that Frank and his bartender, Emil, had to call off all mixed drinks, and serve only straight whiskey and beer.

I have spoken of the actors as hams, and that, unhappily, was what they were, for the Holliday Street was one of the oldest theatres in America, and had long since descended to Theodore Kremer and Charles E. Blaney melodramas. It had a matinée every day (heavily patronized by night-shift street-car conductors and motormen, and their doxies), and before every performance, no matter what the weather, the orchestra, playing as a brass band, performed on the portico over the entrance. This was tough work in Winter, and the work indoors, Winter or no Winter, was almost as onerous, for there was continuous music while a melodrama was going on, and the musicians had to look sharply or miss their cues. The hottest spot was that of Hank Schofield, the bull-fiddler, for on his vigilance depended the success of every scene of lust, vengeance or despair. Whenever the villain was on the stage, which was nearly always, Hank had to accompany his lubricious rascalities *pizzicato*, and when the comic man split his pants the sound had to be caught and augmented *col arco*. Even the love scenes gave Hank no rest, for it was the convention in those days to signalize every kiss

with a jocose *glissando*, and that *glissando* always
started in the bull-fiddle.

Thus Hank was pretty dry by the time the evening performance was over, and nearly every night
he sat at one of Frank's greasy tables with several
other *Tonkünstler* and discussed the decay of their
chosen art. By the time we journalists began to
drop in some of these artists were more or less lit,
and so the evening's ceremonies started off in a very
friendly manner. On our side there was a fixed
ritual. We were organized into a professional society known as the Stevedores' Club (the name, of
course, was a subtle reference to the unloading of
schooners), and as soon as a *minyan* was present
Frank was elected an honorary member. He always received this distinction with modest depre-
cation and embarrassment, and apparently lived
and died without ever figuring out why he got it so
often. But he knew the rule that a new member was
expected to set up the drinks, and in consequence
we always got a round free. Once the experiment
was tried of electing him *twice* in a night, but he
failed to hear the second election, and the scheme
was abandoned. But at about the same time we invented and established a rule that *guests* could
treat the house, though members were forbidden to
do so. The Holliday Street Theatre boys kept this
rule alive by steering in a steady stream of ham
actors, all of whom were welcomed with flattering
speeches. The musicians were not members of the

Stevedores' Club, but when they had a ham in tow
they were free to sit in.

How long the club went on I don't know, for it
was in existence years before my time, and there
were vestiges of it visible so late as 1915, long after
I had become a managing editor and was no longer
eligible. At its peak, say in 1900, it had about a
dozen regular members, and a dozen more who
dropped in off and on. Not only was its direct
patronage valuable to Frank; it also helped him to
wealth by enabling him to stay open beyond the
Baltimore closing hour, which in those days was
midnight. The news of this immunity getting
about, he was soon catering to a large body of miscellaneous night-hawks, including printers, post-
office clerks, bank watchmen, and even street clean-
ers. We objected to the last-named on the ground
of their smell, and they were finally excluded, but
the rest kept coming, and Frank wore out a cash-
register a year ringing up their money. In 1904,
when his place was burned in the great Baltimore
fire, the insurance he received, added to his accumulations, gave him the impressive cash capital of
$175,000, and with it he built a stag hotel and was
quickly rolling in an income even larger than his
old one. Unhappily, his dignity as host of his
hotel required him to wear his Sunday suit every
day, and he soon began to pine away, and was presently no more.

As I have said, it was the presence of the Stevedores' Club that enabled him to keep open after hours, for we journalists naturally had some drag with the cops, and when we represented to Ned Schleigh, their captain in that precinct, that it was inhuman to ask us to clear out at midnight, perhaps in the midst of a belated meal, he allowed that the point was well taken, and instructed his flatfeet to act accordingly. But the reform wave that began to afflict Baltimore at the turn of the century was especially hard on cops, and in 1901 or thereabout a new chief of police took to sending squads of plain-clothes men from remote precincts into the downtown areas of sin, seeking to catch the regular watch in derelictions. One night such a gang of shoo-flies, as they were called, bust into Frank's, and though the members of the Stevedores' Club set up a dreadful bellow, and threatened to break and jail the sergeant in command, Frank got a summons, and we were put to the trouble of having it torn up next morning.

This episode greatly incensed Ned Schleigh, the captain, not only because it revealed to the people of Baltimore a crass violation of the liquor laws in his bailiwick, but also and more especially because it flouted his lawful command and authority. He responded by stationing one of his own cops, in full uniform, at the back door we used for getting in and out of the place, and that cop stood on guard there every night for something on the order of six months, for it took that long for the reform move-

ment to subside. His instructions were to inform
any raiders who showed up that the place was already in the custody of Schleigh himself, who had
raided it only half an hour before. No more appeared, but the six months included a hard February, and the poor cop on duty at the back door,
whose name was Joe, suffered painful frostbites
until his native intelligence suggested that he come
in now and again, and thaw out behind Frank's
stove. Every time he came in he got a shot of Class
C rye, so the arrangement was satisfactory to all
hands. When the reformers were thrown off at
last, and Christian peace and order were restored
in Baltimore, we persuaded the Police Board to
promote Joe to a sergeancy.

Frank, as I have remarked, was a man without
social graces, and it was rare for him to say more
than *Wie geht's* to a customer, whether journalistic or other. But he was highly skilled at his social-
minded craft, and thus enjoyed a kind of esteem
that, in a more responsive man, would have passed
for popularity. He understood very well the principle that a glass of beer running to less than sixteen ounces or costing more than five cents is an
economic atrocity. He also had the acumen to
charge only ten cents for deviled crabs, with an inside rate of five cents to members of the press.
Thus his customers ate well and drank freely, and
in his nightly election to honorary membership in
the Stevedores' Club there was really almost as

much good will as self-interest. When he opened his stag hotel the club followed him, but the place was rather too elegant for the literary trade, and most of the members presently deserted it for the establishment of a compatriot with goat whiskers, known to everyone as Weber and Fields. Weber and Fields was only one man, but no one could make out which of the two comedians he resembled most, so he was named for both. His place was in a dark alley behind the Baltimore *Sun* office, and his small bar was packed every night. He was himself a beer-drinker of great gifts, and was reputed to get down fifty shells a day. The shell he used had a false bottom, but even so his daily ration sounded impressive, and he enjoyed a high degree of public respect.

Those members of the Stevedores' Club who stuck to the splendors of Frank's stag hotel had a somewhat quiet time of it, for the roomers at the place went to bed early, and there was little outside trade in the bar. The bartender, in fact, knocked off every night at midnight, and Frank himself withdrew soon afterward, worn out by the abrasions of his boiled shirt and Sunday suit. This left the main deck in charge of a night-clerk nearly eighty years old, with a young fellow named Rudolph as his only aide. Rudolph served as bell-hop, house dick, and night bartender and oyster-shucker. The night-clerk's faculties were so far clouded by age that he could be disregarded, which

reduced the problem before the club to this: how to
get rid of Rudolph long enough to pillage the bar
and oyster-bar? It was solved night after night by
tipping him off that some member not present had
just sneaked in with a female, and disappeared up
the stairway behind the elevator. This set him to
searching the house, and while he was so engaged a
leisurely burglary was effected. After the fraud
had been worked on him forty or fifty times he began to show signs of tumbling, so the club withdrew. The stag hotel, in fact, was never very popular with the brethren.

But Frank's old place opposite the City Hall
had been their favorite for years, and so long as it
survived it was the home port of all Baltimore
journalists of the malt-liquor moiety. They used,
of course, other saloons — or, as the cops of the
era preferred to call them, kaifs — , but Frank always got them in the end. When his bartender,
Emil, set up business on his own the boys attended
the opening, and some of them dropped in occasionally afterward, but inasmuch as the new establishment was in a remote suburb, half a mile
beyond the rail-head of the nearest trolley line,
getting to it was a fatiguing business. Once, when
Emil threw a party to celebrate the fifth anniver-
sary of the death of Bismarck, the full strength of
the club waited on him, taking along the band of
the Holliday Street Theatre. But when the band
marched up the road from the trolley, playing

brisk Sousa marches, the whole suburb turned out
of bed to hoot and holler, for it was after midnight,
and in those pre-radio days decent people in such
neighborhoods were in the hay by 9:30. The cops
who were summoned joined the party and became
such life as it had, but it never had much, and it was
not repeated.

There were other restauranteurs in the Baltimore of that time who will get friendly notice if
the true history of the town is ever written, which
is, alas, improbable. I remember, for example,
John Roth, who kept a swell place in Fayette street,
next door to the *Herald* office, with a pool parlor
upstairs. He was the *beau idéal* of an old-time
saloonkeeper, with a walrus moustache, a large
paunch, and the manners of an ambassador. He
never went behind his own bar, but always stood in
front of it, near the entrance, so that he could greet
incoming clients. On the wall opposite was the
largest hand-painted oil-painting of Venus rising
from her bath in all the Baltimores. His free lunch
was very well spoken of, and he offered a business
men's lunch at midday that was worth twice its
prix fixe of twenty-five cents. But the best free
lunch of the era was to be had at the Diamond in
Howard street, kept by Muggsy McGraw and Wil-
bert Robinson, two heroes of the old Baltimore
Orioles. Muggsy was too contentious a man to
make a good saloonkeeper, and in a little while he
vanished from the place, but the fat and amiable

Robinson continued on duty for several years, always standing in front of the bar like John Roth. The free lunch at the Diamond was based on an immense chafing-dish of hot dogs, always bubbling, but it also included roast beef, *Schwartenmagen*, and a superior brand of rat-trap cheese. There was a high-toned colored man behind the counter, and any customer of reasonably neat appearance was free to eat all he could hold. The only persons who were barred out as a class, so far as I can recall, were newspaper artists. Robbie had a very low opinion of them, and when one of them wandered in and had to be bounced, he always did it personally.

The most austere restauranteur in Baltimore, and perhaps in the United States, was one Kepler, who kept a place in North street near the City Hall. He was a grave, even sombre man who smiled only once or twice a week. I seldom entered his door, but one snowy night in the Winter of 1900–01 I came near having the honor of being assassinated in front of his bar. The assassin was a minor labor leader who had developed a hate for me because I had written a story revealing him as the caitiff of a fight in a bawdy-house, and he came into the place looking for me, apparently on the mistaken theory that I frequented it. Pulling out two pistols he laid them on the bar, and announced his purpose, naming me by name. Kepler was for trying moral suasion on him, but one of my *Herald* colleagues, who happened to be drinking in the place, preferred more direct action. Seizing a quart bottle of Maryland rye that was on the bar, he brought it down on the labor leader's head, knocking him out at one crack. He then dragged the poor fellow's carcass out into the street, and shoved it into a snow drift. There it lay until the cops came along and sent it to hospital. When, a little while later, I ran into its owner on the street, he seemed to be completely restored, but had no more murder in his heart. The whole thing, he assured me, was a mistake. He was only trying to scare Kepler.

The most hated saloonkeeper in Baltimore in those days — that is, among journalists — was Mike Ganzhorn, who kept a small stag hotel in Baltimore street, with an ornate bar and eating-room downstairs. He was the only member of the whole fraternity who was never, under any circumstances, mentioned in print as a genial restauranteur. Indeed, he never got any mention at all, save only when there was a fight in his bar, or a guest committed suicide upstairs. Mike's crime was that he had once told someone who had told someone who had told someone that he could buy any newspaper man in Baltimore for a drink. This libel rankled for years. It rankled mainly because there was so much truth in it. Mike had taken in slightly too much territory, but there was certainly enough sound ground in the middle to sustain him.

XV

A GIRL FROM

RED LION, P.A.

Somewhere in his lush, magenta prose Oscar
Wilde speaks of the tendency of nature to imitate
art — a phenomenon often observed by persons
who keep their eyes open. I first became aware of
it, not through the pages of Wilde, but at the
hands of an old-time hack-driver named Peebles,
who flourished in Baltimore in the days of this history. Peebles was a Scotsman of a generally un-
friendly and retiring character, but nevertheless
he was something of a public figure in the town.
Perhaps that was partly due to the fact that he had
served twelve years in the Maryland Penitentiary
for killing his wife, but I think he owed much more
of his eminence to his adamantine rectitude in
money matters, so rare in his profession. The very

cops, indeed, regarded him as an honest man, and said so freely. They knew about his blanket refusal to take more than three or four times the legal fare from drunks, they knew how many lost watches, wallets, stick-pins and walking-sticks he turned in every year, and they admired as Christians, though deploring as cops, his absolute refusal to work for them in the capacity of stool-pigeon.

Moreover, he was industrious as well as honest, and it was the common belief that he had money in five banks. He appeared on the hack-stand in front of the old Eutaw House every evening at nine o'clock, and put in the next five or six hours shuttling merrymakers and sociologists to and from the red-light districts. When this trade began to languish he drove to Union Station, and there kept watch until his two old horses fell asleep. Most of the strangers who got off the early morning trains wanted to go to the nearest hotel, which was only two blocks away, so there was not a great deal of money in their patronage, but unlike the other hackers Peebles never resorted to the device of driving them swiftly in the wrong direction and then working back by a circuitous route.

A little after dawn one morning in the early Autumn of 1903, just as his off horse began to snore gently, a milk-train got in from lower Pennsylvania, and out of it issued a rosy-cheeked young woman carrying a pasteboard suitcase and a pink parasol. Squired up from the train-level by a car-greaser with an eye for country beauty, she emerged into the sunlight shyly and ran her eye down the line of hacks. The other drivers seemed to scare her, and no wonder, for they were all grasping men whose evil propensities glowed from them like heat from a stove. But when she saw Peebles her feminine intuition must have told her that he could be trusted, for she shook off the car-greaser without further ado, and came up to the Peebles hack with a pretty show of confidence.

" Say, mister," she said, " how much will you charge to take me to a house of ill fame? "

In telling of it afterward Peebles probably exaggerated his astonishment a bit, but certainly he must have suffered something rationally describable as a shock. He laid great stress upon her air of blooming innocence, almost like that of a cavorting lamb. He said her two cheeks glowed like apples, and that she smelled like a load of hay. By his own account he stared at her for a full minute without answering her question, with a wild stream of confused surmises racing through his mind. What imaginable business could a creature so obviously guileless have in the sort of establishment she had mentioned? Could it be that her tongue had slipped — that she actually meant an employment office, the Y.W.C.A., or what not? Peebles, as he later elaborated the story, insisted that he had cross-examined her at length, and that she had not only reiterated her question in precise terms, but explained that she was fully determined to abandon herself to sin and looked forward confidently to dying in the gutter. But in his first version he reported simply that he had stared at her dumbly until his amazement began to wear off, and then motioned to her to climb into his hack. After all, he was a common carrier, and obliged by law to haul all comers, regardless of their private projects and intentions. If he yielded anything to his Caledonian moral sense it took the form of choosing her destination with some prudence. He might have dumped her into one of the third-rate bagnios that crowded a street not three blocks from Union Station, and then gone on about his business. Instead, he drove half way across town to the high-toned studio of Miss Nellie d'Alembert, at that time one of the leaders of her profession in Baltimore, and a woman who, though she lacked the polish of Vassar, had sound sense, a pawky humor, and progressive ideas.

I had become, only a little while before, city editor of the *Herald*, and in that capacity received frequent confidential communications from her. She was, in fact, the source of a great many useful news tips. She knew everything about everyone that no one was supposed to know, and had accurate advance information, in particular, about Page 1 divorces, for nearly all the big law firms of the town used her facilities for the manufacture of evidence. There were no Walter Winchells in that

era, and the city editors of the land had to depend
on volunteers for inside stuff. Such volunteers
were moved (*a*) by a sense of public duty grace-
fully performed, and (*b*) by an enlightened desire
to keep on the good side of newspapers. Not infrequently they cashed in on this last. I well remember the night when two visiting Congressmen from
Washington got into a debate in Miss Nellie's
music-room, and one of them dented the skull of
the other with a spittoon. At my suggestion the
other city editors of Baltimore joined me in straining journalistic ethics far enough to remove the
accident to Mt. Vernon place, the most respectable
neighborhood in town, and to lay the fracture to a
fall on the ice.

My chance leadership in this public work made
Miss Nellie my partisan, and now and then she
gave me a nice tip and forgot to include the other
city editors. Thus I was alert when she called up
during the early afternoon of Peebles' strange ad-
venture, and told me that something swell was on
ice. She explained that it was not really what you
could call important news, but simply a sort of hu-
man-interest story, so I asked Percy Heath to go to
see her, for though he was now my successor as Sunday editor, he still did an occasional news story, and
I knew what kind he enjoyed especially. He called
up in half an hour, and asked me to join him. " If
you don't hear it yourself," he said," you will say
I am pulling a fake."

When I got to Miss Nellie's house I found her sitting with Percy in a basement room that she used as a sort of office, and at once she plunged into the story.

" I'll tell you first," she began, " before you see the poor thing herself. When Peebles yanked the bell this morning I was sound asleep, and so was all the girls, and Sadie the coon had gone home. I stuck my head out of the window, and there was Peebles on the front steps. I said: ' Get the hell away from here! What do you mean by bringing in a drunk at this time of the morning? Don't you know us poor working people gotta get some rest? ' But he hollered back that he didn't have no drunk in his hack, but something he didn't know what to make of, and needed my help on, so I slipped on my kimono and went down to the door, and by that time he had the girl out of the hack, and before I could say ' scat ' he had shoved her in the parlor, and she was unloading what she had to say.

" Well, to make a long story short, she said she come from somewheres near a burg they call Red Lion, P.A., and lived on a farm. She said her father was one of them old rubes with whiskers they call Dunkards, and very strict. She said she had a beau in York, P.A., of the name of Elmer, and whenever he could get away he would come out to the farm and set in the parlor with her, and they would do a little hugging and kissing. She said Elmer was educated and a great reader, and he would bring her books that he got from his brother, who was a train butcher on the Northern Central, and him and her would read them. She said the books was all about love, and that most of them was sad. Her and Elmer would talk about them while they set in the parlor, and the more they talked about them the sadder they would get, and sometimes she would have to cry.

" Well, to make a long story short, this went on once a week or so, and night before last Elmer come down from York with some more books, and they set in the parlor, and talked about love. Her old man usually stuck his nose in the door now and then, to see that there wasn't no foolishness, but night before last he had a bilious attack and went to bed early, so her and Elmer had it all to theirself in the parlor. So they quit talking about the books, and Elmer began to love her up, and in a little while they was hugging and kissing to beat the band. Well, to make a long story short, Elmer went too far, and when she come to herself and kicked him out she realized she had lost her honest name.

" She laid awake all night thinking about it, and the more she thought about it the more scared she got. In every one of the books her and Elmer read there was something on the subject, and all of the books said the same thing. When a girl lost her honest name there was nothing for her to do excepting to run away from home and lead a life of shame. No girl that she ever read about ever done anything else. They all rushed off to the nearest city, started this life of shame, and then took to booze and dope and died in the gutter. Their family never knew what had became of them. Maybe they landed finally in a medical college, or maybe the Salvation Army buried them, but their people never heard no more of them, and their name was rubbed out of the family Bible. Sometimes their beau tried to find them, but he never could do it, and in the end he usually married the judge's homely daughter, and moved into the big house when the judge died.

" Well, to make a long story short, this poor girl lay awake all night thinking of such sad things, and when she got up at four thirty a.m. and went out to milk the cows her eyes was so full of tears that she could hardly find their spigots. Her father, who was still bilious, give her hell, and told her she was getting her just punishment for setting up until ten and eleven o'clock at night, when all decent people ought to be in bed. So she began to suspect that he may have snuck down during the evening, and caught her, and was getting ready to turn her out of the house and wash his hands of her, and maybe even curse her. So she decided to have it over and done with as soon as possible, and last night, the minute he hit the hay again, she hoofed in to York, P.A., and caught the milk-train for Baltimore, and that is how Peebles found her at Union Station and brought her here. When I asked her what in hell she wanted all she had to say was ' Ain't this a house of ill fame?', and it took me an hour or two to pump her story out of her. So now I have got her upstairs under lock and key, and as soon as I can get word to Peebles I'll tell him to take her back to Union Station, and start her back for Red Lion, P.A. Can you beat it? "

Percy and I, of course, demanded to see the girl, and presently Miss Nellie fetched her in. She was by no means the bucolic Lillian Russell that Peebles' tall tales afterward made her out, but she was certainly far from unappetizing. Despite her loss of sleep, the dreadful gnawings of her conscience and the menace of an appalling retribution, her cheeks were still rosy, and there remained a considerable sparkle in her troubled blue eyes. I never heard her name, but it was plain that she was of four-square Pennsylvania Dutch stock, and as sturdy as the cows she serviced. She had on her Sunday clothes, and appeared to be somewhat uncomfortable in them, but Miss Nellie set her at ease, and soon she was retelling her story to two strange and, in her sight, probably highly dubious men. We listened without interrupting her, and when she finished Percy was the first to speak.

" My dear young lady," he said, " you have been grossly misinformed. I don't know what these works of fiction are that you and Elmer read, but they are as far out of date as Joe Miller's Jest-Book. The stuff that seems to be in them would make even a newspaper editorial writer cough and scratch himself. It may be true that, in the remote era when they appear to have been written, the penalty of a slight and venial slip was as drastic as you say, but I assure you that it is no longer the case. The world is much more humane than it used to be, and much more rational. Just as it no longer burns men for heresy or women for witchcraft, so it has ceased to condemn girls to lives of shame and death in the gutter for the trivial dereliction you acknowledge. If there were time I'd get you some of the more recent books, and point out passages showing how moral principles have changed. The only thing that is frowned on now seems to be getting caught. Otherwise, justice is virtually silent on the subject.

"Inasmuch as your story indicates that no one knows of your crime save your beau, who, if he has learned of your disappearance, is probably scared half to death, I advise you to go home, make some plausible excuse to your pa for lighting out, and resume your care of his cows. At the proper opportunity take your beau to the pastor, and join him in indissoluble love. It is the safe, respectable and hygienic course. Everyone agrees that it is moral, even moralists. Meanwhile, don't forget to thank Miss Nellie. She might have helped you down the primrose way; instead, she has restored you to virtue and happiness, no worse for an interesting experience."

The girl, of course, took in only a small part of this, for Percy's voluptuous style and vocabulary were beyond the grasp of a simple milkmaid. But Miss Nellie, who understood English much better than she spoke it, translated freely, and in a little while the troubled look departed from those blue eyes, and large tears of joy welled from them. Miss Nellie shed a couple herself, and so did all the ladies of the resident faculty, for they had drifted downstairs during the interview, sleepy but curious. The practical Miss Nellie inevitably thought of money, and it turned out that the trip down by milk-train and Peebles' lawful freight of $1 had about exhausted the poor girl's savings, and she had only some odd change left. Percy threw in a dollar and I threw in a dollar, and Miss Nellie not only threw in a third, but ordered one of the ladies to go to the kitchen and prepare a box-lunch for the return to Red Lion.

Sadie the coon had not yet come to work, but Peebles presently bobbed up without being sent for, and toward the end of the afternoon he started off for Union Station with his most amazing passenger, now as full of innocent jubilation as a martyr saved at the stake. As I have said, he embellished the story considerably during the days following, especially in the direction of touching up the girl's pulchritude. The cops, because of their general confidence in him, swallowed his exaggerations, and I heard more than one of them lament that they had missed the chance to handle the case professionally. Percy, in his later years, made two or three attempts to put it into a movie scenario, but the Hays office always vetoed it.

How the girl managed to account to her father for her mysterious flight and quick return I don't know, for she was never heard from afterward. She promised to send Miss Nellie a picture postcard of Red Lion, showing the new hall of the Knights of Pythias, but if it was ever actually mailed it must have been misaddressed, for it never arrived.

XVI

SCIONS OF THE

BOGUS NOBILITY

Of late years, as I have noted in my Preface, American newspaper reporters have come to think of themselves as proletarians, and reach out for communion with coal-miners, truck-drivers, pipe-fitters, bricklayers, and other such wage slaves. It was certainly not so in my early days in the craft. We young journalists, to be sure, were far from snobbish, and in the saloons we frequented we had very amicable relations with various classes of workingmen, notably printers, policemen, musicians and hackmen; nevertheless, we always kept a little distance, and our eyes, when they rolled at all, rolled in the other direction. The hero of our dreams was not Sam Gompers or Gene Debs, but Richard Harding Davis, who was reputed to own twenty suits of clothes, or James Creelman, who had interviewed the Pope. And we were always susceptible to the glamor of less eminent colleagues who had any claim, however false, to high connections, however mysterious. That was a shabby newspaper staff, at least in the big cities, which could not show at least one son of a Civil War general, or nephew of an archbishop, or French count.

In the *Herald* office we had two of the last named, though I should add that neither called himself an actual count. Both were content to let it be known that they were cadets of French families running back to Charlemagne, and would be eating very high on the hog if they could only get their rights. One, when in his cups, spoke of himself as Jean-Baptiste du Plessis de Savines, and the other allowed that he was Jacques de Corbigny. Naturally enough, du Plessis de Savines could not hope to rate his full style and appellation in the turmoil of a newspaper office, so he did not object seriously when Max Ways renamed him Jones. It was a plebeian name — but so, he believed, were all British names. As for Jacques de Corbigny, he was Jake to everyone from Colonel Cunningham down to the office boys, and also to all the functionaries in the Baltimore sties of justice, where he served the *Herald* as court reporter.

Jones oscillated through various jobs in my day, but all of them were of the desk variety, and usually he was telegraph editor. The night report of the Associated Press was then very meagre and in consequence he had a good deal of time on his hands, especially after midnight. In such hours of relaxation he liked to gather a group of young reporters about him, and astonish them with tales of his high doings in a dozen fields of enterprise. He had fought the ten duels that all French counts of his generation had to ring up, and one of them, as the custom provided, was with M. de Blowitz, Paris correspondent of the London *Times*. In addition, he had served his orthodox six years in the Foreign Legion, had escaped in nothing save his pants and hat from an intrigue with a Spanish infanta, had stolen two girls from the Prince of Wales (afterward Edward VII), had climbed the Matterhorn, and had blacked the eyes of both Jake Kilrain and James Gordon Bennett. So far he only ran true to type. But in addition he claimed to be the most adept church organist since Johann Sebastian Bach, and it was in that unusual character that he appeared in some of his most edifying anecdotes.

I well recall one that had to do with his appearance as guest organist at Trinity Church in New York. The news that he was to perform, so he said, brought in such a mob of fans from all over the East that the church was packed. Unhappily, it was discovered at the last minute, just as he was taking off his shoes to fall to, that something was wrong with the organ, and the sexton who usually looked after it not only could not remedy the trouble but even failed to find out what it was. Jones said that his own extraordinarily acute ear solved the mystery at once, though he let the sexton sweat a while in malice: there was something ailing the huge pedal pipe that sounded eighteen octaves below middle C. This pipe was at least two feet in diameter, and its length was such that it ran half way up the steeple. There should have been a manhole in it at the bottom, but Jones could not find one, so while the expectant audience buzzed, scratched itself and blew spitballs, he climbed up to the steeple to look down the open top, as a laryngologist looks down the trachea of a radio crooner.

I shall not detain you with the details: suffice it to say that he lost his balance and plunged headlong down the tube. Fortunately, he was a close fit, so the air was compressed as he went along, and when he landed at last in the conical war-nose of the pipe the jar was no greater than that of a fall on the ice. Nor was there any danger of suffocation, for the organ-pump was still working, and it was easy to turn a stiff breeze into the pipe. But how to get out? Jones confessed that, for a while, he was baffled. He could hear what was going on outside, and he soon picked up the news that the sexton proposed to attempt his rescue with an ax. The rector, it appeared, objected to this, and so did Jones, for he knew the crude technic of sextons, and feared that the ax which liberated him might also decapitate him. In the end he hit on a better scheme, and shouted a command that it be executed. It consisted in sending for riggers, hoisting the pipe out of the steeple, turning it upside down, and then bouncing out Jones on a leaptick of pew-cushions heaped up on the sidewalk.

There were sassy young reporters who refused to believe this story, and some of them asked searching and embarrassing questions, with diagrams designed to show its impossibility, but Jones always stuck to it, and many who doubted when they first heard it came to believe afterward. It was only one chapter in a long saga of his adventures as a performer of sacred music. One of his favorite tricks, he said, was to search out a pipe whose sound made the stained-glass windows of the church vibrate in unison, and then pop them off in the midst of a solemn anthem, to the alarm of the clergy, choir and congregation. He said he had learned how to do this trick with an ordinary parlor, or reed-organ, and once utilized his skill to liberate a baby in arms from a bank vault. The baby's mother, it appeared, had put it in the vault without notifying the bank personnel, and as a result it had been imprisoned when the time-lock clamped down. When Jones was sent for he borrowed an organ from a nearby Sailors' Bethel, found a note in it that would vibrate steel, and so shook the time-lock to pieces. Why the mother had chosen a bank vault for storing her baby, and how she managed to stow it away without being noticed, he did not say.

Toward the end of his life Jones forgot his noble French ancestry, and began shopping around the world for forefathers, and even for fathers. Whenever a bulletin would come in announcing the death of some eminent man he would stagger out into the city room with the Associated Press flimsy, apply his handkerchief to his eyes, and sob piteously. The city editor was then expected to engage him in the following dialogue:

City Editor — What are you blubbering about?

Jones — So-and-so is dead.

City Editor — Well, what of it? What do you care for that ————?

Jones (in a sepulchral whisper) — He — was — my — father.

Everyone would then offer him formal condolences, and he would return to his desk much comforted. Sometimes he would have to be comforted two or three times a week. These raids upon the Christian sympathies of the city editor became so frequent that they irked him, and he terminated them with a bang on the night of November 7, 1901, when news came in of the death of Li Hung Chang. He was aided by a gang of ruffianly copyreaders, organized for the purpose. When Jones appeared with his flimsy and his tears they let fly with ink- and paste-pots, copy-hooks and spittoons. One of them even let go an old typewriter. Jones quit a little while later, and everyone was amazed when word drifted in that he was actually working as organist in a Presbyterian church in a poor suburb — and claiming to be a son of both John Calvin and John Knox.

Jake was a man of more modest pretensions: the most he ever alleged was that his father had been, at one and the same time, a Confederate general, a French nobleman, and a graduate of both Oxford and Cambridge. Unlike Jones, who was very abstemious, Jake was a lusher; indeed, there was a period, say from 1899 to 1902, when he was probably the ranking lusher of the whole region between the Mason & Dixon Line and the James river. He was magnificently ombibulous, drinking anything that contained ethyl alcohol, whatever its flavor or provenance. By day he would sustain himself as court reporter mainly by resorting to the handset whiskey that the printers guzzled at night, and in the evening he would always drop in at Frank Junker's saloon for the session of the Stevedores' Club, with its diligent unloading of schooners of beer. But whenever anything else offered, he got it down, giving thanks to God. Once I saw him drink a quart of apricot brandy at a sitting, and at other times I watched him as he dispatched Angostura, Fernet Branca and Boonekamp bitters by the goblet, all without chasers.

Jake was a tall, sturdy and even herculean fellow, with the wide, confident mouth of a carp or orator, but there came eventually a time when his heroic physique went back on him, and the young doctors at the City Hospital took him on as an out-patient and laboratory animal. So far as I could make out they could never agree on a diagnosis. One held that there was nothing wrong with him save a gastritis so acute that the lining of his stomach had turned to a kind of asphalt, and another that he was in the last stages of cirrhosis of the liver. There were others who voted for Bright's disease, cholelithiasis and scurvy, and a larval psychiatrist held out for paresis, for in those days that malady was still ascribed to drink. Jake himself also favored paresis, for he had noted in his court work that it frequently afflicted distinguished members of the bar. One night he was reciting his symptoms in Junker's when Joe, the cop on the beat, dropped in for his hourly shot of rye, and stood listening in uncomfortable fascination. Finally Joe gave a shiver, and burst out with " Goddam if I don't believe I got the same goddam thing." Jake glared at him for half a minute with singeing scorn, and then replied:

" So you have got paresis, too, have you? A *cop* with paresis? Well, of all the infernal impertinence ever heard of on earth! What ails you, Joe, is *jim-jams*. In order to have paresis you have to have *brains*."

Whatever it was that afflicted Jake, it presently threw him, and he had to be sent to St. Agnes' Hospital, which then specialized in treating the wounded garrison-troops of the Baltimore bar-rooms. The lower floor of the institution, called Hogan's Alley, was always full of them, and Jake found many old friends there, including a rich theatre manager who came down with *mania à potu* twice a year, and always celebrated his cure by giving the good sisters who ran the place some elegant present — one year a *porte cochère*, the next year a new boiler for their heating plant, the third a stained-glass window for their chapel, and so on. There were iron bars on the windows of Hogan's Alley and the inmates lived under rigid discipline, which included complete abstention from alcohol, but they were allowed visitors, were fed upon hearty victuals, and in general led a very easy life.

Jake had a girl known to the boys as the Battleship — a vast, rangy creature built on his own scale, with the broad shoulders and billowing bosoms of a Wagnerian contralto. She came to see him one evening as in duty bound — and an hour later the gentlemen of Hogan's Alley were all full of liquor and cutting wild capers. The sisters, after quieting them, made a search for the source of their supply, but could not find it. Two days later the Battleship made another call — and Hogan's Alley had another too-cheerful night. When it happened a third time the sisters put two and two together, the Battleship was barred from the place, and Jake himself was requested to find some other asylum. They never learned the technic of the smuggling, but Jake himself later revealed it. The Battleship, on each visit, had stowed two quarts of rye between the huge hemispheres of her bosom, and then slipped them quietly to the idol of her dreams, who disposed of them at a dollar a big drink.

Jake's expulsion turned out to be a great stroke of luck for him. The institution he transferred to was a suburban drink-cure run by an enlightened medico who, after curing him, put him to work as a capper in the downtown saloons. All Jake had to do was to keep a sharp lookout for gentlemen showing the first signs of delirium tremens, and report their names to the medico, who thereupon alarmed their families, and usually got them as patients. Jake had comfortable quarters over the dead-house of the drink-cure, and a liberal expense-account. For two or three years he led the life of Riley, and was much envied by all the other boozers of Baltimore. Then, one morning, he dropped dead in a barroom, and was given a neat Odd Fellows funeral by the medico. Some time later a *Herald* reporter digging up a story at the Health Department happened upon Jake's death certificate. It showed that he was born in Philadelphia, that his father's name was something on the order of Schultz, Schmidt or Kraus, and that he had been baptized Emil.

XVII

ALIENS, BUT NOT YET

ENEMIES

THE CURRENT American concept of the German as an excessively sly, bellicose and sinister fellow, apt at any moment to panic the radio audience with false news or blow up a gas-works, was undreamed of in my early days in journalism. We thought of him then as predominantly benignant and not too smart, and that view was fostered by the German reporters who swarmed in all the big cities of the East and Middle West. In every such city there was at least one German daily, with a staff like any other newspaper and not infrequently of considerable importance in local politics. In Baltimore there were two, not to mention four or five weeklies, and on these sheets were some of the most eminent and popular reporters of the town. They covered spot news, to be sure, only sketchily, for a four-alarm fire was nothing to them unless the owner of the burned premises happened to be a German, or, at worst, an Austrian or a Swiss; but ever and anon they had a complicated and hair-raising German suicide to trade for a colored murder, or a riot at a *Gesangverein* rehearsal for a City Hall story, and at all times they were salient figures in what may be called the social life of the Fourth Estate.

If there was any member of our Stevedores' Club who stood out head and shoulders above all the rest of the members, as Ward McAllister rose above the sea-level of the New York 400, then it was certainly John Gfeller of the *Deutsche Correspondent*, a Züricher with a flowing yellow moustache, and a full-dress outfit of frock coat, plug hat and ivory-headed walking-stick that set him off magnificently. Save when he had to cover the wedding of a brewer's daughter or some other such overshadowing and interminable shambles, he showed up at Junker's saloon every night at midnight, and there he led all the other Stevedores in their unloading of schooners. He was the first man of whom I ever heard it said that his legs were hollow, and the last of whom I ever believed it. Malt liquor seemed to have no more effect upon him than so much sarsaparilla, and in all my acquaintance with him I saw him flustered but once, and that was after he had been induced to drink eight or ten mint juleps on a hot July afternoon.

A drinking club always develops a ritual, and the Stevedores' followed the pattern. The basic design of its evening program was simply to shake poor Junker down for free beers, but there was also singing, and in this John naturally led, for he not only had the highest tenor voice in the club, but also a large repertory of robustious songs, most of them relics of his student days in Switzerland. With one or two exceptions the other members knew no more German than so many Irish cops; nevertheless, they learned many of John's songs by rote, as the Welsh and Slovak miners in the Bach Choir at Bethlehem, Pa., learn the Bach cantatas. And even when they were vaguest about the rest of the words they could at least chime in on the choruses, and this they did in voices of brass, always to Junker's alarm, for he lived in fear that, in spite of the immunity the presence of newspaper men was supposed to give him, the cops would clamp down on him for keeping open after hours.

One of the favorites of the club was a song by the celebrated Viktor von Scheffel, whooping up the victory of the primeval Nazis over the Romans under P. Q. Varus in the year 9 A.D. — a victory that threw the Romans over the Rhine for keeps, and made its scene, the Teutoburger Forest, sacred ground in German history. It is now nearly forty years since I last joined in singing this composition, but I remember its opening as clearly as if

John were still uprisen before me, beating time with a foam-scraper:

Als die Römer frech geworden,
Zum, ze rum zum, zum, zum, zum;
Zogen sie nach Deutschland's Norden,
Zum, ze, rum zum, zum, zum, zum.

All the students' *Liederbücher* indicate that every *zum* should have been a *sim*, but in our ignorance we followed John without question, and when we came to the imitation of trumpets in the next strophe we converted them into calliopes, Junker or no Junker, *Polizeistunden* or no *Polizeistunden*. John knew all the seven stanzas, and would sing them with voluptuous gusto, especially the one telling how Varus, in departing swiftly through a swamp, left both of his boots and one of his socks behind, but the rest of us confined ourselves to the choruses, and did not stop to question this somewhat strange account of Roman military costume.

The German reporters led lives that were the admiration of many of their American colleagues, for, as I have said, their papers were not much interested in ordinary news, and there was no court-martial if one of them missed a bank robbery or even a murder, provided, of course, no German were involved. Their main business was to cover the purely German doings of the town — weddings, funerals, concerts, picnics, birthday parties, and so on. This kept them jumping pleasantly, for there were then 30,000 of their compatriots in Baltimore, and most of the 30,000 seemed to be getting on in the world, and were full of social enterprise. It was not sufficient for a German reporter to report their weddings as news : he also had to dance with the bride, drink with her father, and carry off a piece of the wedding cake, presumably for his wife. At a funeral of any consequence — say, that of a saloonkeeper, a pastor, or the head basso of a singing society — his duties were almost as onerous as those of a *Totsäufer* for a brewery,[1] and if he quit before the last clod hit the coffin it was an indecorum. When there were speeches, which was usually, he had to make one, whether at a birthday party, a banquet of the German Freemasons, Knights of Pythias or Odd Fellows, or the opening of a new picnic-grounds, saloon, or Lutheran church. Whenever refreshments were offered, which was always, he had to eat and drink in a hearty and demonstrative manner, and he was remiss in his duties if he failed to sneak in a nice notice for the lady who had prepared the *Sauerbraten* or the *Häringsalat*. In his reports all malt liquor had to be superultra, and all potato salad the best yet seen on earth.

The fattest regular story of the German brethren in my time was the monthly arrival of the North German Lloyd immigrant ship at Locust

---

[1] A *Totsäufer* is a brewery's customers' man. One of his jobs is to weep and beat his breast at the funeral of a saloonkeeper.

Point. All leaves were canceled on that day, and
the instant the ship tied up at the Baltimore & Ohio
pier its decks swarmed with journalists. Even at
the turn of the century, of course, most of the actual immigrants aboard were Slavs or Jews, but
there were still some Germans, and among them
there were bound to be a number of characters
worth embalming in print — say, a barber who had
once shaved Bismarck, or a man with nineteen children, or a Prussian lieutenant whose foot had
slipped in one way or other, forcing him, as the
Germans say, to go 'round the corner. The captain
of the ship always spread a buffet luncheon for the
reporters, and they always got down a couple of
barrels of Munich beer. During his stay in port
the captain would be entertained extensively by the
German societies, for the commander of a North
German Lloyd liner was a notable in all respectable
German circles, and even a young third officer was
a social lion and a swell catch. The German reporters attended all such functions officially, and
stayed until the band went home.

But the story that came nearest to straining
their powers in the days when I knew them best
was the opening of the Anheuser-Busch Brewery's
Baltimore branch in 1900. To cover that historic
event the *Deutsche Correspondent* threw in its
whole local staff, and with them came the chief
editor, an editorial writer, and the circulation manager. How much space the affair got the next

morning I forget, but it must have been many, many columns, despite the fact that several of the older reporters blew up in the course of the evening, and had to be laid out in the cold-storage room to recover. The rival *Journal* not only sent its whole staff but also a photographer. The photographer went down for a count of two or three hundred before he had so much as unlimbered his camera, and was fired on the spot, but when he recovered he rejoined the festivities, and did prodigies with his second wind. A great many reporters from the American papers of Baltimore were also present, and to this day the old-time journalists of the town recall the Anheuser Busch party as indubitably tops in its class. No other brewery ever came within miles of it.

The lordly life of the German colleagues spread the rest of us with the sickly green of envy, but the gods seem to have become envious also, for the great Baltimore fire of 1904 dealt heavy licks to their papers, and World War I finished them. One of the two German dailies succumbed to the first of these calamities, and the other to the second, and all save one of the weeklies went down the chute with the latter. As a result, a great many merry fellows were out of jobs. A few were slipped upon the public payroll by friendly politicians, and a few more managed to make the grade on English newspapers, but the rest had a hard time of it, for their labors, though delightful, had not been lucrative. Indeed, I can recall but one German reporter who ever accumulated any considerable capital, and that one was such a marvel that he was generally regarded as almost inhuman. He was a tall, sallow Oldenburger of the name of Delmenhorst, and in the course of four years' service, at a salary of $15 a week, he saved the neat sum of $16,500. With this he returned to Germany, bought a brickyard in a county town of Brandenburg, and survived into quite modern times — opulent, comfortable, and universally respected.

His wealth, of course, did not flow from his salary: a schoolboy could figure *that*, or even a schoolma'm. He gathered it in simply by turning all the other usufructs of his calling into quick assets. When he went to a German birthday party, and there was on the table a round of *Rinderbrust mit Meerrettig* that met his notions, he not only gobbled down 10,000 or 20,000 calories of it, but lamented loudly that his wife was not present to enjoy it. The hostess, flattered by the encomium of an expert, thereupon always insisted that he take a couple of thick slabs home with him, and in the course of packing them she usually added a bowl of *Bohnensalat*, a chocolate *Torte*, and maybe a bottle of Liebfraumilch or a dozen bottles of beer. Similarly, if paprika chicken was the main dish, he departed with a whole fowl, and if there was roast goose with red cabbage he got enough of each to feed his wife for two or three days.

At the start, so I was told by his fellow-Germans, he confined himself to her actual victualling, but in a little while he began to arrive home with so much provender that she could not get it all down, or even the half of it, so it occurred to him that it might be a good idea for her to take a boarder. The first boarder, a bookkeeper in a sauerkraut factory, put on weight so fast that everyone remarked it, and soon there were eager applications for the second spot. Within a month there were six highly appreciative paying guests at the table, and soon afterward the Delmenhorsts moved to a larger house, put in a colored maid, and increased their clientèle to ten, and then finally to twelve. Simultaneously, they began weeding out such poor fellows as bookkeepers, and substituting bachelors and widowers who could pay better, for example, assistant brewmasters, secretaries of building associations, and interpreters for the North German Lloyd.

Delmenhorst had to sweat hard to round up enough chow for a dozen men. Sometimes he covered eight or ten weddings, birthday parties and other such orgies in an evening, and had a dreadful time promoting a sufficiency of handouts without eating himself to death. But he gradually developed a technic that saved his life, and after a while he hired a colored boy to accompany him from feast to feast with a toy wagon, to haul the loot home. Whenever, by some unhappy accident, there were not enough parties of a night to load the wagon Mrs. Delmenhorst put her boarders on bologna, rat-trap cheese and rye-bread, but that happened very seldom, for the Germans of Baltimore, as I have said, were very social in those days, and loved to stuff their friends. Such wines and beers as he accumulated Delmenhorst sold to the boarders at a discount of twenty per cent., and when his stock began to go beyond their capacity he disposed of the beer to private friends at the same rate, and the wine to the proprietor of a wine-room in East Baltimore.

Nor was it only food and drink that he accumulated. Once a rich baker, celebrating not too quietly the bankruptcy of a rival, gave him a hand-painted oil-painting of the castle at Heidelberg, and he sold it within a week for $17, and another time he wangled a barrel of chinaware from a china-dealer in Gay street. That he ever collected cash was not established to public knowledge, for the matter was naturally kept confidential, but after his return to Germany his old colleagues used to declare that he did, and even professed to know his prices. For an ordinary wedding story, they said, he expected (and usually got) $5, but if it was in moneyed circles, and the bride was so homely that it took some straining of conscience to call her

ravishing, he raised the ante to $10, $15, or $25.
A pious Lutheran, he never charged anything for
funerals, but he would take $5 for a christening,
and when he dealt with a silver or golden wedding
in the upper brackets the sky was the limit. All
saloonkeepers had to pay double, and all brewers
quadruple. Thus, for four years, Delmenhorst
held up the banner of the foreign-language press
in Baltimore, and then, his wife having taken on
such weight that her health broke down, he and she
departed for fresh fields in Brandenburg. They
sailed from Baltimore by the North German
Lloyd, traveling on passes. There was a gaudy
farewell party on the ship — paid for by the line.
For the first time in the four years Delmenhorst
took nothing home from the table.

XVIII

THE SYNTHESIS OF

NEWS

One of the first enemy reporters I came to terms with in the days of my beginnings was an amiable, ribald fellow with a pot belly and a pointed beard, by name Leander J. de Bekker. He hailed from Kentucky by way of Cincinnati and Chicago, and was proud of the fact that he was of Dutch descent. The Dutch, he told me at our first meeting, were the champion beer-drinkers of Christendom, and had invented not only free lunch but also the growler, which got its name, so he said, from the Dutch word *grauw*, signifying the great masses of the plain people. This de Bekker and I made many long and laborious treks together, for he was doing South Baltimore for the *American* when Max Ways sent me there to break in for the *Herald*, and South Baltimore was a vast area of indefinite boundaries and poor communications, with five or six miles of waterfront. At its upper end were the wharves used by the Chesapeake Bay packets, and at its lower end the great peninsula of Locust Point, given over mainly to railroad-yards and grain elevators, but adorned at its nose by Fort McHenry, the bombardment of which in 1814, allegedly by a B——h fleet, inspired Francis Scott Key to write " The Star-Spangled Banner."

There was always something doing in that expansive territory, especially for a young reporter to whom all the major catastrophes and imbecilities of mankind were still more or less novel, and hence delightful. If there was not a powder explosion at Fort McHenry, which was armed with smooth-bore muzzle-loaders dating from 1794, there was sure to be a collision between two Bay packets, and if the cops had nothing in the way of a homicide it was safe to reckon on a three-alarm fire. The blackamoors of South Baltimore were above the common in virulence, and the main streets of their ghetto — York street, Hughsie street and Elbow lane — always ran blood on Saturday nights. It was in Hughsie street, one lovely Summer evening in 1899, that I saw my first murderee — a nearly decapitated colored lady who had been caught by her beau in treason to her vows. And it was in the jungle of warehouses and railroad tracks on Locust Point that I covered my first fire.

De Bekker and I and the reporter for the *Sun-paper* (I forget his name) attended all these public events together, and since de Bekker was the eldest of the trio, and had a beard to prove it, he set the tone and tempo of our endeavors. If, on an expedition to the iron wilds of Locust Point, he decided suddenly that it was time for a hiatus and a beer, we downed tools at once and made for the nearest saloon, which was never more than a block away. Unhappily, the beers of those days, especially along the waterfront, ran only a dozen or so to the keg, and it was thus sometimes difficult for us youngsters, after two or three of them, to throw ourselves into gear again. At such times de Bekker's professional virtuosity and gift for leadership were demonstrated most beautifully.

" Why in hell," he would say, " should we walk our legs off trying to find out the name of a Polack stevedore kicked overboard by a mule? The cops are too busy dragging for the body to ask it, and when they turn it in at last, maybe tomorrow or the day after, it will be so improbable that no union printer in Baltimore will be able to set it up. Even so, they will only guess at it, as they guess at three-fourths of all the names on their books. Moreover, who gives a damn *what* it was? The fact that another poor man has given his life to engorge the Interests is not news: it happens every ten minutes. The important thing here, the one thing that brings us vultures of the press down into this god-forsaken wilderness is that the manner of his death was unusual — that men are not kicked overboard by mules every day. I move you, my esteemed contemporaries, that the name of the deceased be Ignaz Karpinski, that the name of his widow be Marie, that his age was thirty-six, that he lived at 1777 Fort avenue, and that he leaves eleven minor children."

It seemed so reasonable to the *Sun* reporter and me that we could think of no objection, and so the sad facts were reported in all three Baltimore morning papers the next day, along with various lively details that occurred to de Bekker after he had got down another beer. This labor-saving device was in use the whole time I covered South Baltimore for the *Herald*, and I never heard any complaint against it. Every one of the three city editors, comparing his paper to the other two, was surprised and pleased to discover that his reporter always got names and addresses right, and all three of us were sometimes commended for our unusual accuracy. De Bekker, I should add, was a fellow of conscience, and never stooped to what he called faking. That is to say, he never manufactured a story out of the whole cloth. If, under his inspiration, we reported that a mad dog had run amok down the Point and bitten twenty children, there was always an actual dog somewhere in the background, and our count of the victims was at least as authentic as any the cops would make. And if, when an immigrant ship tied up at the North German Lloyd pier, we made it known that fifteen sets of twins had been born during the voyage from Bremen, there were always some genuine twins aboard to support us.

Thus, in my tenderest years, I became familiar with the great art of synthesizing news, and gradually took in the massive fact that journalism is not an exact science. Later, as I advanced up the ladder of the press, I encountered synthesists less conscientious than de Bekker,[1] and indeed became one myself. It was well for me that I showed some talent, else my career might have come to disaster a year or so later, when I was promoted to the City Hall. There I found myself set against two enemy reporters of polished technic and great industry — Frank Kent of the *Sunpaper* and Walter Alexander of the *American*. Kent was a youngster only a little older than I was, but he was a smart fellow, and Alec was already covering his third or fourth city administration, and knew every rat-hole in the City Hall. He remained there for years afterward, and became, in the end, a bottomless abyss of municipal case and precedent. Mayors, comptrollers, health commissioners, city councilmen and other such transient jobholders consulted him as dili-

[1] He left Baltimore in 1901 to join the staff of the Brooklyn *Standard-Union,* and afterward worked for the New York *Tribune* and *Evening Post.* In 1908 he published a dictionary of music, and in 1921 a work on words and phrases in collaboration with Dr. Frank H. Vizetelly, editor of the Standard Dictionary. He died in 1931.

gently as they consulted the daily racing dope. Even in 1900 he knew more than any of them, and was thus a formidable competitor.

Once I had got my legs, Kent and I tried to rope him into a camorra such as de Bekker operated in South Baltimore, but he knew very well that he would contribute a great deal more to its assets than we would, so he played coy, and there was seldom a day that he didn't beat us. One week he let us have it daily with both barrels, and we got into trouble with our city editors. There was, of course, only one remedy, and we were forced into it in haste. Thereafter, we met every afternoon in Reilly's ale-house opposite the City Hall, and concocted a fake to bounce him. That fake appeared the next morning in both the *Sun* and the *Herald*, with refinements of detail that coincided perfectly, so all the city editors of the town, including Alec's, accepted it as gospel. For a week or two Alec tried to blitz and baffle us with real news beats, but when we proceeded from one fake a day to two, and then to three, four, and even more, he came in asking for terms, and thereafter the three of us lived in brotherly concord, with Alec turning up most of the news and Kent and I embellishing it. Our flames of fancy having been fanned, we couldn't shut them off at once, but whenever we thought of a prime fake we let Alec have it also. If it was so improbable that his somewhat literal mind gagged at it we refrained from printing it ourselves, but in such cases we always saved it from going to waste by giving it to the City Hall man of the *Deutsche Correspondent,* a Mannheimer who was ready to believe anything, provided only it was incredible. Once we planted on him an outbreak of yellow fever in the City Jail, but inasmuch as his account of it was printed in German, and buried in columns of gaudy stuff about German weddings, funerals, bowling contests, and other such orgies, our city editors never discovered it.

Kent and I remained in the City Hall about a year, and until the end of that time our relations with Alec were kindly and even loving; in fact, we continued on good terms with him until his lamented death many years afterward. Unhappily, our successors never got next to him as we had, and in consequence he beat them almost every day, and often in a dramatic and paralyzing manner. In the end it was impossible for any rival reporter to stand up to him, and the rich *Sun* had to shanghai him from the poor *American* to avoid disgrace and ruin. More than once Baltimoreans of public spirit, even in the City Hall, proposed that he be elected Mayor himself, and in perpetuity, but like nearly every other good newspaper man, he looked on political office as ignominious, and preferred to remain a reporter. When he died at last the City Hall flag was at half-mast for a week.

The failure of the post-Kent-Mencken flight of City Hall reporters to bring him to a stand as the

Old Masters had done was probably due not only to the natural recession of talent among them, but also to a curious episode that had made a dreadful pother on the *Herald* and was still remembered uneasily by all the journalists of Baltimore. The central figure of that episode was a reporter whose name I shall suppress, for he was unhappily an addict to the hand-set whiskey of the Baltimore printers, and spent a large part of his time sleeping it off in police-stations. Let there be a murder, a fire or even an earthquake, and he would snore through it in one of the roomy barroom chairs that were then provided for the use of professional witnesses, straw bondsmen, and cops on reserve. Max Ways was a man of enlarged views, and had no objection to alcoholism as such, but a narcolept was of little more use to him than a dead man, and one rainy Sunday in the early Winter of 1898–99, being somewhat exacerbated by drink himself, he had the culprit before him, and gave him such a bawling out that even the office boys were aghast.

Moreover, that bawling out was reinforced by an ultimatum. If, by 6 p.m. of that same day, the culprit did not appear in the office with a story worth at least two sticks [2] he was to consider himself fired for the nth and last time, with no hope of appeal, pardon, commutation or reprieve, whether in this world or the next. The poor fish, alarmed,

[2] A stick is about two inches of type.

shuffled off to police headquarters and begged the cops to help him, but they reported that the bleak, filthy weather had adjourned all human endeavor in the town, and that they had nothing in hand save two lost colored children and a runaway horse. He then proceeded to such other public offices as were open, but always he met with the same response. Somewhere or other he picked up the death of a saloonkeeper, but the saloonkeeper was obscure, and thus worth, at most, only a few lines. It began to look hopeless, and he slogged on despairingly, soaked by the rain and scarcely knowing where he was going.

This woeful tramp took him at last to the shopping district, and he started to plod it just as dusk was coming down. Simultaneously, the arc-lights which, in that era, hung outside every store of any pretensions began to splutter on, and in his gloomy contemplation of them he was suddenly seized with an idea — the first, in all likelihood, that had occurred to him for long months, and maybe even years. Those arc-lights were above the range of pedestrians on the sidewalks, but it would be easy to reach any of them with an umbrella. Suppose a passer-by carrying a steel-rodded umbrella should lift it high enough to clear another passer-by's umbrella, and its ferrule should touch the steel socket that held the lower carbon of one of the lights, and suppose there should be some leakage of electricity, and it should shoot down the umbrella rod, and

into the umbrella's owner's arm, and then, facili-
tated by his wet clothes, down his legs and into the
sidewalk — what would be the effect upon the man?
The speculation was an interesting one, and the
poor fish paused awhile to revolve it in his deterio-
rated mind.

The next morning the *Herald* printed a story
saying that a man named William T. Benson, aged
forty-one, a visitor from Washington, had made
the experiment accidentally in West Baltimore
street, and had been knocked, figuratively speaking, into a cocked hat. There was a neat description of the way the current had thrown him half
way across the street, and a statement from him
detailing his sensations *en route*. He had not, he
said, lost consciousness, but gigantic pinwheels in
all the colors of the rainbow whirled before his eyes,
and in the palm of his right hand was a scarlet
burn such as one might pick up by grasping a red-
hot poker. Moreover, his celluloid collar had been
set to smoking, and might have burst into flames
and burned his neck if a stranger had not rushed
up and quenched it with his handkerchief. The
young doctors at the University Hospital, so it appeared, regarded Mr. Benson's escape alive as almost miraculous, and laid it to the fact that he had
rubber heels on his shoes. Fortunately, their science was equal to the emergency, and they predicted that their patient would be as good as new,
save for his burned hand, by morning. But they

trembled to think of the possible fate of the next victim.

This story, which ran well beyond two sticks and rated a display head, saved the narcolept's job — but only temporarily. By ten o'clock the next morning more than 200 Baltimore merchants had called up the electric company and ordered the lights in front of their stores taken away at once. By noon the number was close to a thousand, and by 3 p.m. the lawyers of the electric company were closeted with Nachman, the business manager of the *Herald*, and his veins were running ice-water at their notice of a libel suit for $500,000. They were ready to prove in court, they said, that it was as impossible to get a shock from one of their lights as from a child's rattle. The whole apparatus was fool, drunk, boy, idiot, suicide, and even giraffe proof. It had been tested by every expert in the nation, and pronounced perfect.

What became of the poor fish no one ever learned, for he got wind of the uproar before coming to the office the next day, and in fact never came at all, but vanished into space. The check-up that went on, with half the staff thrown into it, produced only misery of a very high voltage. The cops knew nothing of any such accident, the doctors at the University Hospital had no record of it, and the only William T. Benson who could be found in Washington had not been in Baltimore for nine years. Nor was there any lifting of the gloom when the *Herald's* own lawyer was consulted. This gentleman (he afterward reached the eminence of a Federal circuit judge) was one of those old-fashioned attorneys who saw every case as lost, and liked to wring their clients' hearts. If the *Herald* went into court, he said, he would have to stand mute, for there was no conceivable defense, and if it offered a compromise the electric company would be insane to take anything less than $499,999.99. The most that could be hoped for was that a couple of implacable utilities-haters would sneak past the company's fixers and get on the jury, and there scale down the damages to something less brutal — say $250,000 or $300,-000.

During the month following the *Herald* printed twenty or thirty news stories acknowledging and denouncing the fake, and at least a dozen editorials apologizing for it, but many of the merchants had become immovably convinced that what could be imagined might some day actually happen, so the revenues of the electric company continued depleted, and the bellowing of its lawyers broke all records. When the case was finally set down for an early trial every *Herald* man felt relieved, for it was clearly best to get the agony over, go through a receivership, and start anew. On the day before the day of fate there was really a kind of gaiety in the office. Once more it was raining dismally, but everyone was almost cheerful. That afternoon a man carrying a steel-rodded umbrella lifted it to clear another pedestrian's umbrella in West Baltimore street, and the ferrule touched the lower carbon-socket of one of the few surviving arc-lights. When the cops got him to hospital he was dead.

I tell the tale as it was told to me: it all happened before I joined the staff. My own talent for faking fell into abeyance after I left the City Hall, and especially after I became city editor. In that office, in fact, I spent a large part of my energy trying to stamp it out in other men. But after I was promoted to managing editor, it enjoyed a curious recrudescence, and my masterpiece of all time, with the sole exception of my bogus history of the bathtub, printed in the New York *Evening Mail* on December 28, 1917, was a synthetic war dispatch printed in the *Herald* on May 30, 1905. The war that it had to do with was the gory bout between Japan and Russia, and its special theme was the Battle of Tsushimi or Korea Straits, fought on May 27 and 28. Every managing editor on earth knew for weeks in advance that a great naval battle was impending, and nearly all of them had a pretty accurate notion of where it would be fought. Moreover, they all began to get bulletins, on May 27, indicating that it was on, and these bulletins were followed by others on the day following. They came from Shanghai, Hongkong, Foochow and all the other ports of the China coast. They were set in large type and printed under what were

then called stud-horse heads, but they really offered nothing better than rumors of rumors.
Everyone knew that a battle was being fought, and
everyone assumed that the Japanese would win,
but no one had anything further to say on the subject. The Japs kept mum, and so did the Russians.

Like any other managing editor of normal appe-
tites I was thrown into a sweat by this uncertainty.
With the able aid of George Worsham, who was
then news editor of the *Herald*, I had assembled a
great array of cuts and follow stuff to adorn the
story when it came, and though the *Herald* had
changed to an evening paper by that time, he and
I remained at our posts until late in the evenings
of May 27 and 28, hoping against hope that the
story would begin to flow at any minute, and give
us a chance to bring out a hot extra. But nothing
came in, and neither did anything come in on May
29 — that is, nothing save more of the brief and
tantalizing bulletins from the China coast. On the
evening of this third day of waiting and lathering
I retired to my cubby-hole of an office — and wrote
the story in detail. The date-line I put on it was
the plausible one of Seoul, and this is how it began:

From Chinese boatmen landing upon the Korean coast
comes the first connected story of the great naval battle
in the Straits of Korea on Saturday and Sunday.

After that I laid it on, as they used to say in
those days, with a shovel. Worsham read copy on

me, and contributed many illuminating details. Both of us, by hard poring over maps, had accumulated a knowledge of the terrain that was almost fit to be put beside that of a China coast pilot, and both of us had by heart the names of all the craft in both fleets, along with the names of their commanders. Worsham and I worked on the story until midnight, and the next morning we had it set in time for our noon edition. It began on Page 1 under a head like a fire-alarm, jumped double-leaded to Page 2, and there filled two and three-quarters columns. It described in throbbing phrases the arrival of the Russians, the onslaught of the Japs, the smoke and roar of the encounter, and then the gradual rolling up of the Jap victory. No one really knew, as yet, which side had won, but we took that chance. And to give verisimilitude to our otherwise bald and unconvincing narrative, we mentioned every ship by name, and described its fate, sending most of the Russians to the bottom and leaving the field to Admiral Count Heihachiro Togo. With it we printed our largest, latest and most fierce portrait of the admiral, a smaller one of his unhappy antagonist, Admiral Zinivy Petrovitch Rozhdestvensky, and a whole series of pictures of the contending ships, with all the Russian marked either " damaged " or "sunk."

Thus the *Evening Herald* scored a beat on the world, and, what is more, a beat that lasted for nearly two weeks, for it took that long for any authentic details of the battle to reach civilization. By that time, alas, our feat was forgotten — but not by its perpetrators. Worsham and I searched the cables from Tokyo, when they began to come in at last, with sharp eyes, for we lived in fear that we might have pulled some very sour ones. But there were no such sour ones. We had guessed precisely right in every particular of the slightest importance, and on many fine points we had even beaten the Japs themselves. Years later, reading an astonishing vivid first-hand account of the battle by an actual participant, Aleksei Silych Novikov,[3] I was gratified to note that we were still right.

[3] Translated as Tsushima; New York, 1937.

XIX

FIRE ALARM

AT midnight or thereabout on Saturday, February 6, 1904, I did my share as city editor to put the *Sunday Herald* to bed, and then proceeded to Junker's saloon to join in the exercises of the Stevedores' Club. Its members, having already got down a good many schooners, were in a frolicsome mood, and I was so pleasantly edified that I stayed until 3:30. Then I caught a night-hawk trolley-car, and by four o'clock was snoring on my celibate couch in Hollins street, with every hope and prospect of continuing there until noon of the next day. But at 11 a.m. there was a telephone call from the *Herald* office, saying that a big fire had broken out in Hopkins Place, the heart of downtown Baltimore, and fifteen minutes later a reporter dashed up to the house behind a sweating hack horse, and rushed in with the news that the fire looked to be a humdinger, and promised swell pickings for a

dull Winter Sunday. So I hoisted my still malty
bones from my couch and got into my clothes, and
ten minutes later I was on my way to the office with
the reporter. That was at about 11:30 a.m. of
Sunday, February 7. It was not until 4 a.m. of
Wednesday, February 10, that my pants and shoes,
or even my collar, came off again. And it was not
until 11:30 a.m. of Sunday, February 14 — precisely a week to the hour since I set off — that I got
home for a bath and a change of linen.

For what I had walked into was the great Baltimore fire of 1904, which burned a square mile out
of the heart of the town and went howling and
spluttering on for ten days. I give the exact schedule of my movements simply because it delights
me, in my autumnal years, to dwell upon it, for it
reminds me how full of steam and malicious animal
magnetism I was when I was young. During the
week following the outbreak of the fire the *Herald*
was printed in three different cities, and I was present at all its accouchements, herding dispersed and
bewildered reporters at long distance and cavorting gloriously in strange composing-rooms. My
opening burst of work without a stop ran to sixty-
four and a half hours, and then I got only six hours
of nightmare sleep, and resumed on a working
schedule of from twelve to fourteen hours a day,
with no days off and no time for meals until work
was over. It was brain-fagging and back-break-
ing, but it was grand beyond compare — an adven-

ture of the first chop, a razzle-dazzle superb and elegant, a circus in forty rings. When I came out of it at last I was a settled and indeed almost a middle-aged man, spavined by responsibility and aching in every sinew, but I went into it a boy, and it was the hot gas of youth that kept me going. The uproar over, and the *Herald* on an even keel again, I picked up one day a volume of stories by a new writer named Joseph Conrad, and therein found a tale of a young sailor that struck home to me as the history of Judas must strike home to many a bloated bishop, though the sailor naturally made his odyssey in a ship, not on a newspaper, and its scene was not a provincial town in America, but the South Seas. Today, so long afterward, I too "remember my youth and the feeling that will never come back any more — the feeling that I could last forever, outlast the sea, the earth, and all men . . . Youth! All youth! The silly, charming, beautiful youth!"

Herald reporters, like all other reporters of the last generation, were usually late in coming to work on Sundays, but *that* Sunday they had begun to drift in even before I got to the office, and by one o'clock we were in full blast. The fire was then raging through a whole block, and from our fifth-floor city-room windows it made a gaudy show, full of catnip for a young city editor. But the Baltimore firemen had a hundred streams on it, and their chief, an old man named Horton, reported that they would knock it off presently. They might have done so, in fact, if the wind had not changed suddenly at three o'clock, and begun to roar from the West. In ten minutes the fire had routed Horton and his men and leaped to a second block, and in half an hour to a third and a fourth, and by dark the whole of downtown Baltimore was under a hail of sparks and flying brands, and a dozen outlying fires had started to eastward. We had a story, I am here to tell you! There have been bigger ones, of course, and plenty of them, but when and where, between the Chicago fire of 1871 and the San Francisco earthquake of 1906, was there ever one that was fatter, juicier, more exhilarating to the journalists on the actual ground? Every newspaper in Baltimore save one was burned out, and every considerable hotel save three, and every office building without exception. The fire raged for a full week, helped by that bitter Winter wind, and when it fizzled out at last the burned area looked like Pompeii, and up from its ashes rose the pathetic skeletons of no less than twenty overtaken and cremated fire-engines — some of them from Washington, Philadelphia, Pittsburgh and New York. Old Horton, the Baltimore fire chief, was in hospital, and so were several hundred of his men.

My labors as city editor during that electric week were onerous and various, but for once they did not include urging lethargic reporters to step into it. The whole staff went to work with the enthusiasm of crusaders shinning up the walls of Antioch, and all sorts of volunteers swarmed in, including three or four forgotten veterans who had been fired years before, and were thought to have long since reached the dissecting-room. Also, there were as many young aspirants from the waiting-list, each hoping for his chance at last, and one of these, John Lee Blecker by name, I remember brilliantly, for when I told him to his delight that he had a job and invited him to prove it he leaped out with exultant gloats — and did not show up again for five days. But getting lost in so vast a story did not wreck his career, for he lived to become, in fact, an excellent reporter, and not a few old-timers were lost, too. One of the best of them, sometime that afternoon, was caught in a blast when the firemen began dynamiting buildings, and got so coagulated that it was three days before he was fit for anything save writing editorials. The rest not only attacked the fire in a fine frenzy, but also returned promptly and safely, and by four o'clock thirty typewriters were going in the city-room, and my desk was beginning to pile high with red-hot copy.

Lynn Meekins, the managing editor, decided against wasting time and energy on extras: we got out one, but the story was too big for such banalities: it seemed like a toy balloon in a hurricane. " Let us close the first city edition," he said,

" at nine o'clock. Make it as complete as you can. If you need twenty pages, take them. If you need fifty, take them." So we began heaving copy to the composing-room, and by seven o'clock there were columns and columns of type on the stones, and picture after picture was coming up from the engraving department. Alas, not much of that quivering stuff ever got into the *Herald*, for a little before nine o'clock, just as the front page was being made up, a couple of excited cops rushed in, howling that the buildings across the street were to be blown up in ten minutes, and ordering us to clear out at once. By this time there was a fire on the roof of the *Herald* Building itself, and another was starting in the press-room, which had plate-glass windows reaching above the street level, all of them long ago smashed by flying brands. We tried to parley with the cops, but they were too eager to be on their way to listen to us, and when a terrific blast went off up the street Meekins ordered that the building be abandoned.

There was a hotel three or four blocks away, out of the apparent path of the fire, and there we went in a dismal procession — editors, reporters, printers and pressmen. Our lovely first edition was adjourned for the moment, but every man-jack in the outfit believed that we'd be back anon, once the proposed dynamiting had been done — every man-jack, that is, save two. One was Joe Bamberger, the foreman of the composing-room, and the other was Joe Callahan, my assistant as city editor. The first Joe was carrying page-proofs of all the pages already made up, and galley-proofs of all the remaining type-matter, and all the copy not yet set. In his left overcoat pocket was the front-page logotype of the paper, and in his left pocket were ten or twelve halftones. The other Joe had on him what copy had remained in the city-room, a wad of Associated Press flimsy about the Russian-Japanese war, a copy-hook, a pot of paste, two boxes of copy-readers' pencils — and the assignment-book!

But Meekins and I refused to believe that we were shipwrecked, and in a little while he sent me back to the *Herald* Building to have a look, leaving Joe No. 2 to round up such reporters as were missing. I got there safely enough, but did not stay long. The proposed dynamiting, for some reason unknown, had apparently been abandoned, but the fire on our roof was blazing violently, and the press-room was vomiting smoke. As I stood gaping at this dispiriting spectacle a couple of large plate-glass windows cracked in the composing-room under the roof, and a flying brand — some of them seemed to be six feet long! — fetched a window on the editorial floor just below it. Nearly opposite, in Fayette street, a sixteen-story office building had caught fire, and I paused a moment more to watch it. The flames leaped through it as if it had been made of matchwood and drenched with gasoline, and in half a minute they

were roaring in the air at least 500 feet. It was,
I suppose, the most melodramatic detail of the
whole fire, but I was too busy to enjoy it, and as I
made off hastily I fully expected the whole struc-
ture to come crashing down behind me. But when
I returned a week later I found that the steel frame
and brick skin had both held out, though all the
interior was gone, and during the following Summer the burned parts were replaced, and the building remains in service to this day, as solid as the
Himalayas.

At the hotel Meekins was trying to telephone to
Washington, but long-distance calls still took time
in 1904, and it was fifteen minutes before he raised
Scott C. Bone, managing editor of the Washington *Post*. Bone was having a busy and crowded
night himself, for the story was worth pages to
the *Post*, but he promised to do what he could for
us, and presently we were hoofing for Camden Station, a good mile away — Meekins and I, Joe Bamberger with his salvage, a copy-reader with the salvage of the other Joe, half a dozen other desk men,
fifteen or twenty printers, and small squads of
pressmen and circulation men. We were off to
Washington to print the paper there — that is, if
the gods were kind. They frowned at the start, for
the only Baltimore & Ohio train for an hour was
an accommodation, but we poured into it, and by
midnight we were in the *Post* office, and the hospitable Bone and his men were clearing a place for

us in their frenzied composing-room, and ordering the press-room to be ready for us.[1]

Just how we managed to get out the *Herald* that night I can't tell you, for I remember only trifling details. One was that I was the principal financier of the expedition, for when we pooled our money at Camden Station it turned out that I had $40 in my pocket, whereas Meekins had only $5, and the rest of the editorial boys not more than $20 among them. Another is that the moon broke out of the Winter sky just as we reached the old B. & O. Station in Washington, and shined down sentimentally on the dome of the Capitol. The Capitol was nothing new to Baltimore journalists, but we had with us a new copy-reader who had lately come in from Pittsburgh, and as he saw the matronly dome for the first time, bathed in spooky moonlight, he was so overcome by patriotic and aesthetic sentiments that he took off his hat and exclaimed " My God, how beautiful! " And a third is that we all paused a second to look at the red glow over Baltimore, thirty-five miles away as the crow flies. The fire had really got going by now, and for four nights afterward the people of Washington could see its glare from their streets.

Bone was a highly competent managing editor, and contrived somehow to squeeze us into the tu-

[1] Bone was an Indianan, and had a long and honorable career in journalism, stretching from 1881 to 1918. In 1919 he became publicity chief of the Republican National Committee, and in 1921 he was appointed Governor of Alaska. He died in 1936.

multous *Post* office. All of his linotypes were already working to capacity, so our operators were useless, but they lent a hand with the make-up, and our pressmen went to the cellar to reinforce their *Post* colleagues. It was a sheer impossibility to set up all the copy we had with us, or even the half of it, or a third of it, but we nevertheless got eight or ten columns into type, and the *Post* lent us enough of its own matter to piece out a four-page paper. In return we lent the hospitable *Post* our halftones, and they adorned its first city edition next morning. Unhappily, the night was half gone before Bone could spare us any press time, but when we got it at last the presses did prodigics, and at precisely 6.30 the next morning we reached Camden Station, Baltimore, on a milk-train, with 30,-000 four-page *Heralds* in the baggage-car. By 8 o'clock they were all sold. Our circulation hustlers had no difficulty in getting rid of them. We had scarcely arrived before the news of our coming began to circulate around the periphery of the fire, and in a few minutes newsboys swarmed in, some of them regulars but the majority volunteers. Very few boys in Baltimore had been to bed that night: the show was altogether too gaudy. And now there was a chance to make some easy money out of it.

Some time ago I unearthed one of these orphan *Heralds* from the catacombs of the Pratt Library in Baltimore, and gave it a looking-over. It turned out to be far from bad, all things considered. The story of the fire was certainly not complete, but it was at least coherent, and three of our halftones adorned Page 1. The eight-column streamer-head that ran across its top was as follows:

HEART OF BALTIMORE WRECKED BY
GREATEST FIRE IN CITY'S HISTORY

Well, brethren, what was wrong about that? I submit that many worse heads have been written by pampered copy-readers sitting at luxurious desks, with vassals and serfs at their side. It was simple; it was direct; there was no fustian in it; and yet it told the story perfectly. I wrote it on a make-up table in the *Post* composing-room, with Meekins standing beside me writing a box for the lower right-hand corner of the first page, thanking the *Post* for its " proverbial courtesy to its contemporaries " and promising formally that the *Herald* would be "published daily by the best means it can command under the circumstances."

Those means turned out, that next day, to be a great deal short of ideal. Leaving Joe Callahan, who had kept the staff going all night, to move to another and safer hotel, for the one where we had found refuge was now in the path of the fire, Meekins and I returned to Washington during the morning to make arrangements for bringing out a larger paper. We were not ashamed of our four pages, for even the *Sunpaper*, printed by the Washington *Evening Star,* had done no better, but what were four pages in the face of so vast a story? The boys had produced enough copy to fill at least ten on the first day of the fire, and today they might turn out enough to fill twenty. It would wring our gizzards intolerably to see so much good stuff going to waste. Moreover, there was art to consider, for our two photographers had piled up dozens of gorgeous pictures, and if there was no engraving plant left in Baltimore there were certainly plenty in Washington.

But Bone, when we routed him out, could not promise us any more accommodation than he had so kindly given us the first night. There was, it appeared, a long-standing agreement between the *Post* and the Baltimore *Evening News,* whereby each engaged to take care of the other in times of calamity, and the *News* staff was already in Washington cashing in on it, and would keep the *Post* equipment busy whenever it was not needed by the *Post* itself. Newspapers in those days had no such plants as they now boast: if I remember rightly, the *Post* had not more than a dozen linotypes, and none of them could chew up copy like the modern monsters. The prospect seemed depressing, indeed, but Bone himself gave us a shot of hope by mentioning casually that the Baltimore *World* appeared to have escaped the fire. The *World?* It was a small, ill-fed sheet of the kind then still flourishing in most big American cities, and its own daily editions seldom ran beyond four pages, but it was an *afternoon* paper, and we might hire its equipment for the night. What if it had only four linotypes? We might help them out with hand-set matter. And what if its Goss press could print but 5,000 six- or eight-page papers an hour? We might run it steadily from 6 p.m. to the middle of the next morning, bringing out edition after edition.

We got back to Baltimore as fast as the B. & O. could carry us, and found the *World* really unscathed, and, what is more, its management willing to help us, and as soon as its own last edition was off that afternoon Callahan and the gentlemen of the *Herald* staff came swarming down on its little office in Calvert street. The ensuing night gave me the grand migraine of my life, with throbs like the blows of an ax and continuous pinwheels. Every conceivable accident rained down on us. One of the linotypes got out of order at once, and when, after maddening delays, Joe Bamberger rounded up a machinist, it took him two hours to repair it, and even then he refused to promise that it would work. Meekins thereupon turned to his desperate plan to go back to Gutenberg and set matter by hand — only to find that the *World* had insufficient type in its cases to fill more than a few columns. Worse, most of this type appeared to be in the wrong boxes, and such of it as was standing on the stones had been picked for sorts by careless printers, and was pretty well pied.[2]

Meekins sent me out to find more, but all the larger printers of Baltimore had been burned out, and the only supply of any size that I could discover was in the office of the *Catholic Mirror*, a weekly. Arrangements with it were made quickly, and Joe Bamberger and his gallant lads of the union rushed the place and proceeded to do or die, but setting type by hand turned out to be a slow and vexatious business, especially to linotype operators who had almost forgotten the case. Nor did it soothe us to discover that the *Mirror's* stock of type (most of it old and worn) was in three or four different faces, with each face in two or three sizes, and that there was not enough of any given face

[2] Perhaps I should explain some printers' terms here. The stones are flat tables (once of actual stone, but now usually of steel) on which printers do much of their work. Type is kept in wooden cases divided into boxes, one for a character. As it is set up by the compositor it is placed in galleys, which are brass frames, and then the galleys are taken to the stone and there made up. Sometimes, after the printing has been done, the type is returned to a stone, and left there until a convenient time to return it to the cases. To pick sorts is to go to such standing type and pick out characters that are exhausted in the cases. Pied type is type in such confusion that it cannot be returned to the cases by the usual method of following the words, but must be identified letter by letter. To forget the case, mentioned below, is to lose the art of picking up types from the boxes without looking at them. The boxes are not arranged alphabetically, and a printer learns the case as one learns the typewriter keyboard. A face of type is a series of sizes of one design. The face in which this line is set is called Scotch Modern and the size is eight point. The text above is in eleven and one-half point Scotch Modern.

and size to set more than a few columns. But it was
now too late to balk, so Joe's goons went to work,
and by dark we had ten or twelve columns of copy
in type, some of it in eight-point, some in ten-
point and some in twelve-point. That night I rode
with Joe's chief of staff, Josh Lynch, on a comman-
deered express-wagon as these galleys of motley
were hauled from the *Mirror* office to the *World*
office. I recall of the journey only that it led down
a steep hill, and that the hill was covered with ice.
Josh howled whenever the horse slipped, but somehow or other we got all the galleys to the *World*
office without disaster, and the next morning, after
six or eight breakdowns in the pressroom, we came
out with a paper that at least had some news in it,
though it looked as if it had been printed by country printers locked up in a distillery.

When the first copy came off the *World's* rickety
Goss press Meekins professed to be delighted with
it. In the face of almost hopeless difficulties, he
said, we had shown the resourcefulness of Robinson
Crusoe, and for ages to come this piebald issue of
the *Herald* would be preserved in museums under
glass, and shown to young printers and reporters
with appropriate remarks. The more, however, he
looked at it the less his enthusiasm soared, and
toward the middle of the morning he decided suddenly that another one like it would disgrace us
forever, and announced at once that we'd return to
Washington. But we knew before we started that

the generous Bone could do no more for us than he
had already done, and, with the *Star* monopolized
by the Baltimore *Sun,* there was not much chance
of finding other accommodation in Washington
that would be better than the *World's* in Baltimore.
The pressure for space was now doubled, for not
only was hot editorial copy piling up endlessly,
but also advertising copy. Hundreds of Baltimore
business firms were either burned out already or
standing in the direct path of the fire, and all of
them were opening temporary offices uptown, and
trying to notify their customers where they could
be found. Even in the ghastly parody printed in
the *World* office we had made room for nearly three
columns of such notices, and before ten o'clock
Tuesday morning we had copy for ten more.

But where to turn? Wilmington in Delaware?
It was nearly seventy miles away, and had only
small papers. We wanted accommodation for
printing ten, twelve, sixteen, twenty pages, for the
Herald had suffered a crippling loss, and needed
that volunteer advertising desperately. Philadelphia? It seemed fantastic, for Philadelphia was
nearly a *hundred* miles away. To be sure, it had
plenty of big newspaper plants, but could we bring
our papers back to Baltimore in time to distribute
them? The circulation men, consulted, were optimistic. " Give us 50,000 papers at 5 a.m.," they
said, " and we'll sell them." So Meekins, at noon or
thereabout, set off for Philadelphia, and before

dark he was heard from. He had made an arrangement with Barclay H. Warburton, owner of the Philadelphia *Evening Telegraph*. The *Telegraph* plant would be ours from 6 p.m., beginning tomorrow, and it was big enough to print any conceivable paper. Meekins was asking the Associated Press to transfer our report from Baltimore to Philadelphia, and the International Typographical Union to let our printers work there. I was to get out one more edition in Washington, and then come to Philadelphia, leaving Callahan in charge of our temporary office in Baltimore. But first I was to see Oscar G. Murray, president of the B. & O. Railroad, and induce him to give us a special train from Philadelphia to Baltimore, to run every night until further notice.

The B. & O.'s headquarters building in Baltimore had been burned out like the *Herald* office, but I soon found Murray at Camden Station, functioning grandly at a table in a storage warehouse. A bachelor of luxurious and even levantine tastes, he was in those days one of the salient characters of Baltimore, and his lavender-and-white striped automobile was later to become a major sight of the town. When he gave a party for his lady friends at the Stafford Hotel, where he lived and had his being, it had to be covered as cautiously as the judicial orgies described in Chapter XII. He looked, that dreadful afternoon, as if he had just come from his barber, tailor and haberdasher. He was shaved so closely that his round face glowed like a rose, and an actual rose was in the buttonhole of his elegant but not too gaudy checked coat. In three minutes I had stated my problem and come to terms with him. At two o'clock, precisely, every morning a train consisting of a locomotive, a baggage-car and a coach would be waiting at Chestnut Street Station in Philadelphia, with orders to shove off for Baltimore the instant our *Heralds* were loaded. It would come through to Camden Station, Baltimore, without stop, and we could have our circulation hustlers waiting for it there.

That was all. When I asked what this train would cost, the magnificent Murray waved me away. " Let us discuss that," he said, " when we are all back home." We did discuss it two months later — and the bill turned out to be nothing at all. " We had some fun together," Murray said, " and we don't want to spoil it now by talking about money." That fun consisted, at least in part, of some very exuberant railroading. If we happened to start from Philadelphia a bit late, which was not infrequent as we accumulated circulation, the special train made the trip to Baltimore at hair-raising speed, with the piles of *Heralds* in the baggage-car thrown helter-skelter on the curves, and the passengers in the coach scared half to death. All known records between Philadelphia and Baltimore were broken during the ensuing five weeks. Finally the racing went so far beyond the seemly that the proper authorities gave one of the engineers ten days lay-off without pay for wild and dangerous malpractice. He spent most of his vacation as the guest of our printers in Philadelphia, and they entertained him handsomely.

But there was still a paper to get out in Washington, and I went there late in the afternoon to tackle the dismal job. The best Bone could do for us, with the Baltimore *News* cluttering the *Post* office all day and the *Post* itself printing endless columns about the fire still raging, was four pages, and of their thirty-two columns nearly thirteen were occupied by the advertisements I have mentioned. I got the business over as soon as possible, and returned to Baltimore eager for a few winks of sleep, for I had not closed my eyes since Sunday morning, and it was now Wednesday. In the *Herald's* temporary office I found Isidor Goodman, the night editor. He reported that every bed in downtown Baltimore was occupied two or three deep, and that if we sought to go home there were no trolley-cars or night-hacks to haul us. In the office itself there was a table used as a desk, but Joe Callahan was snoring on it. A dozen other men were on the floor.

Finally, Isidor allowed that he was acquainted with a lady who kept a surreptitious house of assignation in nearby Paca street, and suggested that business was probably bad with her in view of the competing excitement of the fire, and that she might be able in consequence to give us a bed. But when we plodded to her establishment, which was in a very quiet neighborhood, Isidor, who was as nearly dead as I was, pulled the wrong door-bell, and a bass voice coming out of a nightshirt at a second-story window threatened us with the police if we didn't make off. We were too tired to resist this outrage, but shuffled down the street, silent and despairing. Presently we came to the Rennert Hotel, and went in hoping to find a couple of vacant spots, however hard, on a billiard-table, or the bar, or in chairs in the lobby. Inside, it seemed hopeless, for every chair in sight was occupied, and a dozen men were asleep on the floor. But there was a night-clerk on duty whom we knew, and after some mysterious hocus-pocus he whispered to us to follow him, and we trailed along up the stairs to the fourth floor. There he unlocked a door and pointed dramatically to a vacant bed, looking beautifully white, wide and deep. We did not wait to learn how it had come to be so miraculously vacant, but peeled off our coats and collars, kicked off our shoes, stepped out of our pants, and leaped in. Before the night-clerk left us we were as dead to this world and its sorrows as Gog and Magog. It was 4 a.m. and we slept until ten. When we got back to the *Herald's* quarters we let it be known that we had passed the night in the house of Isidor's friend in Paca street, along with two rich society women from Perth Amboy, N.J.

That night we got out our first paper in Philadelphia — a gorgeous thing of fourteen pages, with twenty columns of advertising. It would knock the eyes out of the *Sun* and *Evening News*, and we rejoiced and flapped our wings accordingly. In particular, we were delighted with the *Evening Telegraph's* neat and graceful head-type, and when we got back to Baltimore we imitated it. Barclay Warburton, the owner of the *Telegraph*, came down to the office to see us through — elegantly invested in a tail coat and a white tie. Despite this unprofessional garb, he turned out to be a smart fellow in the pressroom, and it was largely due to his aid that we made good time. I returned to Baltimore early in the morning on the first of Oscar Murray's special trains, and got a dreadful bumping on the curves and crossings. The circulation boys fell on our paper with exultant gurgles, and the next night we lifted the press-run by 10,000 copies.

We stayed in Philadelphia for five weeks, and gradually came to feel almost at home there — that is, if anybody not born in the town can ever feel at home in Philadelphia. The attitude of the local colleagues at first puzzled us, and then made us snicker in a superior way. Save for Warburton himself, not one of them ever offered us the slightest assistance, or, indeed, even spoke to us. We were printing a daily newspaper 100 miles from base — a feat that remains unparalleled in Amer-

ican journalism, so far as I know, to this day —
and it seemed only natural that some of the Philadelphia brethren should drop in on us, if only out
of curiosity. But the only one who ever appeared
was the managing editor of one of the morning
papers, and he came to propose graciously that we
save him a few dollars by lending him our halftones of the fire. Inasmuch as we were paying his
paper a substantial sum every day for setting ads
for us — the *Evening Telegraph* composing-room
could not handle all that crowded in — we replied
with a chilly nix, and he retired in a huff.

There was a press club in Philadelphia in those
days, and its quarters downtown offered a convenient roosting-place for the hour or two after the
night's work was done. In any other American
city we'd have been offered cards on it instantly
and automatically, but not in Philadelphia. At the
end of a week a telegraph operator working for us
got cards for us in some unknown manner, and a
few of us began using the place. During the time
we did so only one member ever so much as spoke to
us, and he was a drunken Englishman whose conversation consisted entirely of encomiums of Barclay Warburton. Whenever he saw us he would
approach amiably and begin chanting "Good ol'
Bahclay! Good ol' Bahclay! Bahclay's a good
sawt," with *sawt* rhyming with *caught*, and apparently meaning *sort*. We agreed heartily, but suffered under the iteration, and presently we forsook

the place for the saloon patronized by the *Herald* printers, where there was the refined entertainment described in Chapter XI.

Meekins's arrangements for getting out the *Herald* so far from home were made with skill and worked perfectly. Callahan remained in Baltimore in charge of our field quarters outside the burned area, and on every train bound for Philadelphia during the afternoon he had an office-boy with such copy as had accumulated. At six o'clock, when the *Evening Telegraph* men cleared out of their office, we opened a couple of private wires, and they kept us supplied with later matter. Even after the fire burned out at last Baltimore was in an appalling state, and there were plenty of old Baltimoreans who wagged their heads despairingly and predicted that it would never be rebuilt. One such pessimist was the Mayor of the town: a little while later, yielding to his vapors, he committed suicide. But there were optimists enough to offset these glooms, and before we left Philadelphia the debris was being cleared away, many ancient and narrow streets were being widened, and scores of new buildings were started. All these debates and doings made for juicy news, and the men of the local staff, ably bossed by Callahan, poured it out daily. Meekins would come to Philadelphia two or three times a week to look over his faculty in exile, and I would drop down to Baltimore about as often to aid and encourage Joe. We had our

own printers in Philadelphia and our own pressmen. Our circulation department performed mar-
vels, and the advertising department gobbled up
all the advertising in sight, which, as I have said,
was plenty. The *Herald* had been on short com-
mons for some time before the fire, but during the
two or three months afterward it rolled in money.

Once I had caught up on lost sleep I prepared
to do a narrative of the fire as I had seen it, with
whatever help I could get from the other *Herald*
men, but the project got itself postponed so often
that I finally abandoned it, and to this day no connected story has ever been printed. The truth is
that, while I was soon getting sleep enough, at least
for a youngster of twenty-four, I had been depleted by the first cruel week more than I thought,
and it was months before I returned to anything
properly describable as normalcy. So with the rest
of the staff, young and old. Surveying them when
the hubbub was over, I found confirmation for my
distrust, mentioned in Chapter XI, of alcohol as a
fuel for literary endeavor. They divided themselves sharply into three classes. Those who had
kept off the stuff until work was done and it was
time to relax — there were, of course, no all-out teetotalers in the outfit — needed only brief holidays
to be substantially as good as new. Those who had
drunk during working hours, though in modera-
tion, showed a considerable fraying, and some of
them had spells of sickness. Those who had boozed

in the classical manner were useless before the end of the second week, and three of them were floored by serious illnesses, one of which ended, months later, in complete physical and mental collapse. I pass on this record for what it is worth.

XX

SOLD DOWN THE

RIVER

AFTER five weeks in Philadelphia we moved back
to Baltimore. The steel skeleton of the *Herald*
Building was still standing, and it might have been
furnished with a new skin and viscera as the other
burned office-buildings of Baltimore were furnished, but the city had seized it to widen a street,
and the place where it stood soon became the Courthouse Plaza, which is today given over to parked
automobiles. I had visited its ruins a number of
times during the month after the fire, and once
shinned up its shell to the fifth floor, and investi-
gated the mortal remains of the editorial rooms.
It was easy to find the place where my desk had
stood, though the desk itself was only a heap of
white dust, for its hardware survived and so did the

frame of the goose-neck light that had stood upon
it. I also found my old copy-hook, twisted as if it
had died in agony, and I have it yet. But all the
clippings and other records that had stuffed the
drawers of the desk were gone, and I thus lost many
souvenirs of my earliest days, including a collection of pieces of hangmen's ropes. In that era the
sheriff pontificating at a Maryland hanging always cut up the rope afterwards to give to his fans,
and the reporters on hand were included. If my
collection had survived I suppose I'd have presented it, soon or late, to the Smithsonian, but it is
no more, and I do not repine.

The indefatigable Meekins, with such help as he
could squeeze out of Peard, the general manager,
had leased an old car-barn in South Charles street,
just outside the area of the fire, and there he set up
fifteen or twenty linotypes, and a second-hand Hoe
press that he had found in New York. I have seen
much worse newspaper offices in my time. At the
start the editorial rooms were in a little three-story
building across an alley from the barn, but that
turned out to be an inconvenient arrangement, and
we soon moved into the barn itself, which was wide
and deep. This put the whole operation of the
paper, from the writing and editing of copy to the
printing and delivery, on one floor — a scheme
that has been adopted deliberately, in recent years,
by a number of mid-Western dailies that happened
to have room enough for it. We got out a pretty

good paper, and circulation showed some gains, but the post-fire burst of advertising did not last, and by the beginning of Summer the *Herald* was in difficulties. The advertising trend, even in those days, was away from morning papers, and it was especially marked in Baltimore, where the *Evening News*, published by Charles H. Grasty, was making inroads on the morning *Sun*. In the morning field we had not only the *Sun* to face, but also the *American;* in the evening field there was nothing beside the *News* save the *World*, which had hardly any advertising at all.

So Peard decided to switch from morning to evening — and then, at the last moment, had an attack of caution, and ordered Meekins to keep the morning going until we could make out how the evening was doing. It was characteristic of that well-meaning but highly unjournalistic man that he never stopped to figure out how one staff could produce two papers. Not a single extra man was hired. Meekins was managing editor of both, and I was city editor of both. This preposterous arrangement went on for a single week, and then we all blew up. During that week I never got home at all, but slept, when I slept at all, on a couch in the office — usually from 2 a.m. to 6 or 7. It was the end of August, 1904, in sticky Summer weather, and the car-barn was only a block from the waterfront, in the hottest part of Baltimore. Changes of clothes were sent to me from home, but the only baths I got were from a fire-hose in the press-room.

Launched under such disadvantages, the *Evening Herald* was naturally something of a scarecrow, and its reception by the gentry and commonalty of Baltimore was far from enthusiastic. Grasty's *Evening News* was then, as always, a bad newspaper, but it was not quite as bad as the *Evening Herald*, and the advertisers of the town showed no sign of deserting him to fatten us. Peard and his men in the business office tried to put all the blame on the editorial department, but we bit and scratched back, and after an insane week of his noble experiment the morning *Herald* was abandoned, and we began to get out an evening edition that looked more or less like a newspaper. But the Sunday morning paper was continued, and so my work-day on Saturday ran from 7 a.m. to 1 or 2 a.m. Sometimes I was able to snatch a nap in the afternoon, but more often I was not, and the thing I principally remember about the time is that I always slept so late on Sunday morning that I was unable to sleep Sunday night, and that it commonly took me until Wednesday to oscillate back to my normal hours. We all sweated and schemed, but it gradually became plain that without fresh money and new and wonder-working management the *Herald* was doomed. Natural forces were also in operation against us, for the great reduction in the number of American daily papers that marked the 20's and 30's was already beginning. Baltimore had five in 1904, and in 1903 it had had six, but today it has but three.

In the midst of these dismal struggles, at some time or other in 1905, Meekins's title was changed to that of editor-in-chief, and I was made managing editor in his place, with Joe Callahan succeeding me as city editor. It was a step that must have caressed inevitably the gills of any youngster of twenty-five, for though I was well aware of the *Herald's* gloomy prospects, it was nevertheless a daily newspaper, and in a city of more than 500,-000 people. Most of my fellow-freshmen of 1899 were still reporters, and some were out of jobs, but here was I, by the sheer power of a singular virtue, rising to great and puissant dignities, and ready to become (as I suspected) the Ajax of a new crop of legends as astonishing as those which swathed Cunningham, Carter and Meekins himself. It was a great day when I overheard an office-boy speak of me, to a colleague, as the Old Man, and another when the office stationery came back from the printers with Meekins's name blacked out and mine printed above it. But as the duties of my new office took me deeper and deeper into the affairs of the paper I became better and better aware of its parlous state. Meekins told me daily of his palavers with Peard and with Oler, the iceman who owned the paper, and what he had to report was predominantly depressing. On those rare days when news came down from the business office uptown that a

new 300-line ad had been snared he and I would go
to Joyce's Hotel opposite Camden Station and
blow ourselves to a swell dinner.

It would be an error, however, to say that I was
ever despondent, or anything remotely resembling
it. I was still only twenty-five — and at twenty-
five the hot ichor of youth is still roaring in the
veins. I argued, even against the wise Meekins,
that the paper could still be saved, and both of us
certainly shirked no blood and sweat to that end.
Having no responsibility for the editorial page, I
leaped from crag to crag in the news department,
and kept a constant eye on composing-room and
press-room. If a desk man was out of service I took
over his duties for the day; if there was a rush of
business in the city-room I sat in as an extra copy-
reader; once, for a month running, I got out the
woman's page; and whenever Meekins was off the
job I lent a hand with the editorial page. It was a
busy and exhilarating life, despite all the lugubrious bulletins from the front office, and I enjoyed
it immensely. But all the while, I am sure, I was
accumulating a conviction that executive posts
were not for Henry, and formulating plans, if only
unconsciously, to avoid them in the still dim future.
Meekins himself, as I have said in Chapter IX,
probably contributed more to that determination
than either he or I realized at the time.

I recall, in point, the day when the proofs of my
first real book, " George Bernard Shaw: His

306

Plays," came in. It was a small volume, else I could not have found the time to write it at all, but it was nevertheless a book, set up and to be published by a real publisher, and I was so enchanted that I could not resist taking the proofs to the office and showing them to Meekins — on the pretense, as I recall, of consulting him about a doubtful passage. He seemed almost as happy about it as I was. " If you live to be two hundred years old," he said, " you will never forget this day. It is one of the great days of your life, and maybe the greatest. You will write other books, but none of them will ever give you half the thrill of this one. Go to your office, lock the door, and sit down to read your proofs. Nothing going on in the office can be as important. Take the whole day off, and enjoy yourself." I naturally protested, saying that this or that had to be looked to. " Nonsense! " replied Meekins. " Let all those things take care of themselves. I *order* you to do nothing whatsoever until you have finished with the proofs. If anything pops up I'll have it sent to *me*." So I locked myself in as he commanded, and had a shining day indeed, and I can still remember its unparalleled glow after all these years.

On January 20, 1906, there was a mysterious confab in the business office uptown, and the next day the *Herald* announced that " at a meeting of the board of directors of the *Herald* Publishing Company the resignation of Mr. Frank F. Peard as president and general manager was received with regret." On the same day Meekins appeared on the flagstaff of the paper as president and publisher, and under his name was this:

Henry L. Mencken, *Secretary and Editor*

The details of Peard's exitus I never heard, and in fact I never inquired about them. He was always extremely polite to me, but my communion with him had early convinced me that his talents, however distinguished, did not lie in the newspaper field. He had many other irons in the fire, and at one time made a weekly trip to New York to function as secretary of a typewriter company. The only part of the paper that he showed any genuine interest in was the financial page. To embellish it he saddled us with a stock tipster who used the *nom de plume* of G. de Baldevinus — an amiable old fellow who was well liked in the office, but guessed wrong almost as often as our racing tipster. Baldevinus did all his work in the composing-room, where he used one of the stones as a desk, and in the course of an average afternoon he would receive six or eight telephone calls from Peard, who played the stock market steadily, and lost nine times out of ten.

Both Peard and Oler were naturally fertile in editorial ideas, all of them bad. Whenever Oler sent in a request that something be printed about himself or one of his friends the resultant copy was

marked " Ice," which was our ground-rules equivalent of the usual newspaper " Must." I can recall
forlorn days when the city-room copy-hook was
almost choked with " Ice " stuff. Peard's orders
were quite as numerous, and even more demoraliz-
ing. Once, at Christmas time, he let the advertising manager of a Baltimore department-store sell
him the notion that it would be fine propaganda for
the *Herald* if we could induce every trolley passenger to add a penny to his nickel fare, as a Christmas offering to the conductors. A smart reporter
was assigned to work up the idea, and he did it in
a series of stories full of sly satire that Peard swallowed without suspicion. Some of the conductors
threw the pennies in the passengers' faces, for that
was before effective fare-registers had been invented, and any conductor with his wits about him
was a man of means, for he could easily knock down
five times his wages. Others got into rows with their
motormen, who tried to muscle in on the swag —
which never, I believe, amounted to anything. We
received hundreds of letters denouncing us as
rogues and imbeciles, mainly on the ground that
giving money to the conductors would only incite
the trolley monopoly to cut their wages.

Peard was always an easy mark for press-
agents, and especially for those representing what
he regarded as prospective advertisers. It would
be unjust to blame him here, for we were desperately in need of more lineage, but his seductions

were often very embarrassing to the editorial department. More than once a good reporter, assigned to write some extravagant piece of balderdash, bucked violently and threatened to resign. Inasmuch as I always sympathized with him heartily, I was debarred from putting any pressure on him, and had to resort to cajolery. Even nonadvertisers found Peard willing and eager — for example, the Christian Scientists. That was in the days before the late Charles Scribner had given them a salutary trouncing in the matter of the E. F. Dakin book on Ma Eddy, which they tried in vain to suppress. In every American city they had a committee on publication which roved the newspaper offices, confidently demanding space for the lectures of their traveling exegetes. When they first appeared in the *Herald* office I threw them out, but they soon came back with a chit from Peard, and for a couple of years we had to make room for their nonsense. The copy-desk struck back by converting it into even worse nonsense, and by writing idiotic heads on it, so I had to watch it carefully.

But now Peard had faded out at last,[1] and Meekins was in full charge of the paper, with only Oler over him. I was secretary of the company, but so far as I can recall there was never any meeting of the board; in fact, I never heard the names of the members thereof, if any. Meekins's prin-

[1] In his later years he made a considerable success in the insurance business in California, and died there in 1925.

cipal job was to blackjack money out of the reluctant and now terrified Oler. He was successful for a few months, but after that Oler began to dry up, for he had become convinced at last that his political career was under the curse of God. In the early Spring of 1906 a number of the larger advertisers of Baltimore, concluding that it might be good *Geschäft* to keep the *Evening Herald* alive, if only for use as a club against Grasty and his *Evening News*, appeared with an offer to chip in enough to meet our weekly deficits. Meekins and I added a bottle of claret to our dinner at Joyce's that night, but when the advertisers began to mention actual money it appeared that the best they were willing to do was far short of our needs, and after some vain gabble they took to the woods. From that time onward it was only a matter of standing the death-watch. Finally, on June 17, we printed the following on the editorial page:

NOTICE

Tomorrow the property of the *Herald* Publishing Company will pass into new hands, and there will be no further publication of the *Sunday Herald,* the *Evening Herald,* or the *Weekly Herald.*

" New hands " was something of a euphemism. We had virtually nothing to sell, for all our mechanical equipment was mortgaged, and our morning Associated Press membership, save for the Sunday edition, had been forfeited by our switch to the evening field. Nevertheless, the other Baltimore papers seem to have put up a nominal sum to get rid of the wreck, for I discovered years later, on searching the corporation records of the Baltimore *Sun*, that its share had been $3,125. The staff, during the last year, had gradually reduced itself, for everyone suspected what was coming, and at the time of the final crack no one was much perturbed, at any event in the editorial department. Nearly all the boys found new jobs without difficulty, some in Baltimore and the rest in other cities, and those who didn't went into other trades. Joe Callahan, the city editor, started a weekly paper for builders and contractors that still survives and is still prosperous, though Joe himself is long dead.

As for me, I was, like Meekins, in apparent difficulties, for it is a newspaper maxim that when a paper blows up the chances of its hirelings landing new jobs run in inverse proportion to their rank. The office-boys are at work again the next day, and good reporters are snapped up quickly, but managing editors are out on a limb, for vacancies in their gloomy trade come rarely and are usually filled by promotion, and if they look for lesser posts they encounter the same prejudice that afflicts ex-managers in the theatre. But I was lucky, for all three of the larger dailies of Baltimore offered me jobs, and I took the first offer that reached me. It came from Grasty of the *Evening News:* he wanted me to be his news editor. But after a couple of weeks in the job I decided finally that executive work was not to my taste, and in a little while I transferred to the *Sunpaper* as Sunday editor, a more leisurely and literary job. Soon I was set to writing editorials, and after that my contributions to the various *Sunpapers* — morning, evening and Sunday — were destined to go on with only an occasional break until the early days of 1941. Since 1910, save for a brief and unhappy interlude in 1938, I have never had a newspaper job which involved the control of other men's work, or any responsibility for it.

Library of Congress Cataloging-in-Publication Data

Mencken, H. L. (Henry Louis), 1880-1956.
   Newspaper Days, 1899-1906 / H. L. Mencken.—Maryland paperback
bookshelf ed.
     p.   cm.—(Maryland paperback bookshelf)
   Originally published : New York : Knopf, 1941.
   ISBN 0-8018-5340-0 (alk. paper)
   1. Mencken, H. L. (Henry Louis), 1880-1956—Knowledge—Communications.
   2. Newspaper editors—Maryland—Baltimore—Biography. 3. Journalists—
Maryland—Baltimore—Biography. 4. Authors, American—20th century—
Biography. 5. Baltimore (Md.)—Newspapers—History. 6. Baltimore
(Md.)—Biography. I. Title. II. Series.
PS3525.E43Z47 1996
818'.5209—dc20

                                                        95-52240